THIS IS OUR WORLD

THE REVOLUTIONARY AGE

First published in this edition 1976
Published by William Collins Sons and Company Limited, Glasgow and London
© 1976 illustrations L'Esperto S.p.A., Milan and Tradexim S.A., Geneva
© 1976 English language text William Collins Sons and Company Limited
Printed in Great Britain
ISBN 0 00 106125 9

THIS IS OUR WORLD

THE REVOLUTIONARY AGE

by Ann Currah

Foreword by James Burke

Collins

Glasgow and London

Contents

Foreword	6
Introduction	7

The Seeds of Revolution — 8
Nobility's gates	8
Washing on the line	11
First moves	12
Wigs thrown away	14
Breaking the symbol of power	16
What Paris wants, France will have	18
The people feel power	21
Restricting privelege	23
The days of terror	25
From citizen to emperor	27
A hen looking after her brood	28
The brilliant general	30
Cutting Britain off	32
Shearing grass	35
Defeat at last	36
Power and glory left behind	38
The final defeat	40

A New Age Begins — 42
Peace and order	42
Cobwebs on crowns	44
Patching up the leaks	46
Ideas in the wind	49
Chopping up the old powers	50
The citizen-king	52
Sitting on a time bomb	55
Red ivy	56
The agrarian revolution	59
Working life changes	60
Water power	62
From water to coal	64
Swallowing up the people	66
From legs to wheels	68
Tools make slums	70
Telephone business	72

Men and Ideas — 75
A new idol	76
Light and dark	78

Power and pleasure	81
The brain and the pen	82
People in books	84
The hooded falcon	86
A new kind of European	88
The people's friend in royal robes	90
The second Empire	93
Man of accidents	95
The new package	96
The hand on the controls	98
The final blow	101

A Nation Grows 102
Frontier lands	105
People power	107
Cotton fights brick	108
The growth of industry	110
Yearning to be free	112
Progress speeds up	114
The bogey-man will get you!	116
Children's life	118
The table of society	121

Slums of progress	123
Clean and healthy	124
Crime and punishment	127
A new luxury	128
The specialist	130
Scientific magic	133
Man studies mankind	134
Survival of the fittest	136
Free or muzzled?	138
Climb aboard!	140
Carried on the tide	142

The Gravy Train 145
Britons round the world	146
New subjects	148
Spreading civilization	150
Guns and goods	152
Fledglings trying to fly	155
A nest of hope	156

Index 158

Foreword

We live, today, in a world of unparalleled complexity. The flow of information that ought to make that complexity comprehensible has reached the proportions of an uncontrollable torrent. National libraries are unable to say how much is being written, or by whom. The computer has so far been unable to produce a means of providing the general public with access to the information. And yet, access to it becomes more vital, as knowledge becomes more and more specialized.

As the log jam builds up, the development of telecommunications, particularly in the form of television, presents the young people of today with glimpses of a world that their parents already find difficult to cope with. There is increasing concern among the older generation about the need for the kind of information that will enable them to understand and if necessary argue with the changes brought about daily by new developments. It is not that the new knowledge has been deliberately withheld—rather that comprehension demands an ever-increasing expertise in the basic elements of a bewildering number of disciplines.

Again and again in my work I receive letters from parents, and even teachers, asking where they can find the facts that will permit them to explain to their children and pupils why change occurs, and what effects change will have. To such letters, the only possible answer is "read". And yet, where do you go to read, when so many of the thousands of fragmented groups of scientists and thinkers find it so difficult to explain to each other what it is they are doing? There is urgent need, at the adult level, for some kind of common source of data, provided in some common language. Researchers are at present working on such a new language—it's called a meta-language—to answer the problem of translating from English to English.

The dilemma has occurred with the dramatic increase in the sheer number of "things known" over the last half-century. Someone recently said about today's world: "if you understand something it must be obsolete". That is the nub of the problem. The world moves too fast, in too many directions, for anyone to really know more than a tiny fraction of everything there is to know, in any depth. The task, for the adult, is possibly hopeless.

All the more reason that the present-day system of education, which must inevitably equip a child for a career by encouraging specialization, should provide tomorrow's specialist with as wide a grounding in knowledge as possible. It is only with such a broad preparation that tomorrow's specialist will stand a chance of communicating to his fellow members of society. That is why I commend this particular work. It covers an enormously wide variety of subjects, from the nervous system to Alexander the Great and beyond the earth to the stars. Above all, the text is written in such a way as to benefit maximally from use of the way a *child* sees the world. The illustrations are admirably clear, and facts are presented in analogies that a child would use. The work is, I think, a successful attempt to provide easily absorbed, and more important, easily memorable explanations of the world around us. It provides a valuable base on which a young mind can build.

James Burke

Introduction

This book and the companion volumes present a bold, clear picture of the knowledge man has gained about himself, his earth, and the universe he lives in. The text is aimed particularly at young readers of about nine years and upwards.

Here we discuss many important aspects of civilization and history in the latter part of the eighteenth century, and in the nineteenth century. From the French Revolution, to the rise of Napoleon, to the new industrial society which began in the century before our own, man's way of life changed profoundly. The invention of steam-powered engines, and later the invention of the telephone and the telegraph meant that people and countries were no longer isolated. Better transport and means of communicating brought people throughout the world closer together.

Young readers' knowledge of these events in man's history is naturally limited. Helping children to draw on and to learn new information using their own memories and experiences is of great importance in their understanding of man's history.

As we all realize, the simple accumulation of dates, names, places and events can no longer be a major aim of learning. What children today need is to be able to adapt to changing states of knowledge, to be able to re-learn and re-think throughout adult life. This encyclopedia sets out to help children to learn to think for themselves. The means employed are simple.

The pictures are large, colourful, specially planned photographs and related drawings. The idea behind them is to draw on children's own knowledge to explain ideas, and to begin to put historical concepts in perspective. For example, we all know that Napoleon was an extraordinarily brilliant military commander. The picture used on page 33 to accompany the text about Napoleon's soldierly genius shows a computer riding on a white horse. The idea may seem unusual to adults, but children will readily make the connection that men in Napoleon's time stood in awe of his command of detail and facts, just as today we marvel at a computer's ability to pour forth facts and details.

Seeds of Revolution

Nobility's gates

By the second half of the eighteenth century, France was the most advanced country in Europe. It had more people, all governed by one ruler, than any other country. All things French were very fashionable. In most European countries, educated men and women spoke French to show they were in fashion and were educated.

But society in France was more backward than in many other European countries. The people belonged to one of three estates (or classes). The First Estate was made up of churchmen. The Second Estate were noblemen and noblewomen—the aristocracy. The Third Estate included everyone else, from tradesmen to starving beggars. The Second Estate knew very little about the everyday life of the Third Estate. They did not know that men, women and children were starving. They did not realize that commoners wanted a change in society. The French nobility lived peacefully and gaily, tucked away in their big houses, not knowing that the time was coming when the Third Estate would storm their gates and demand more justice and a better way of life.

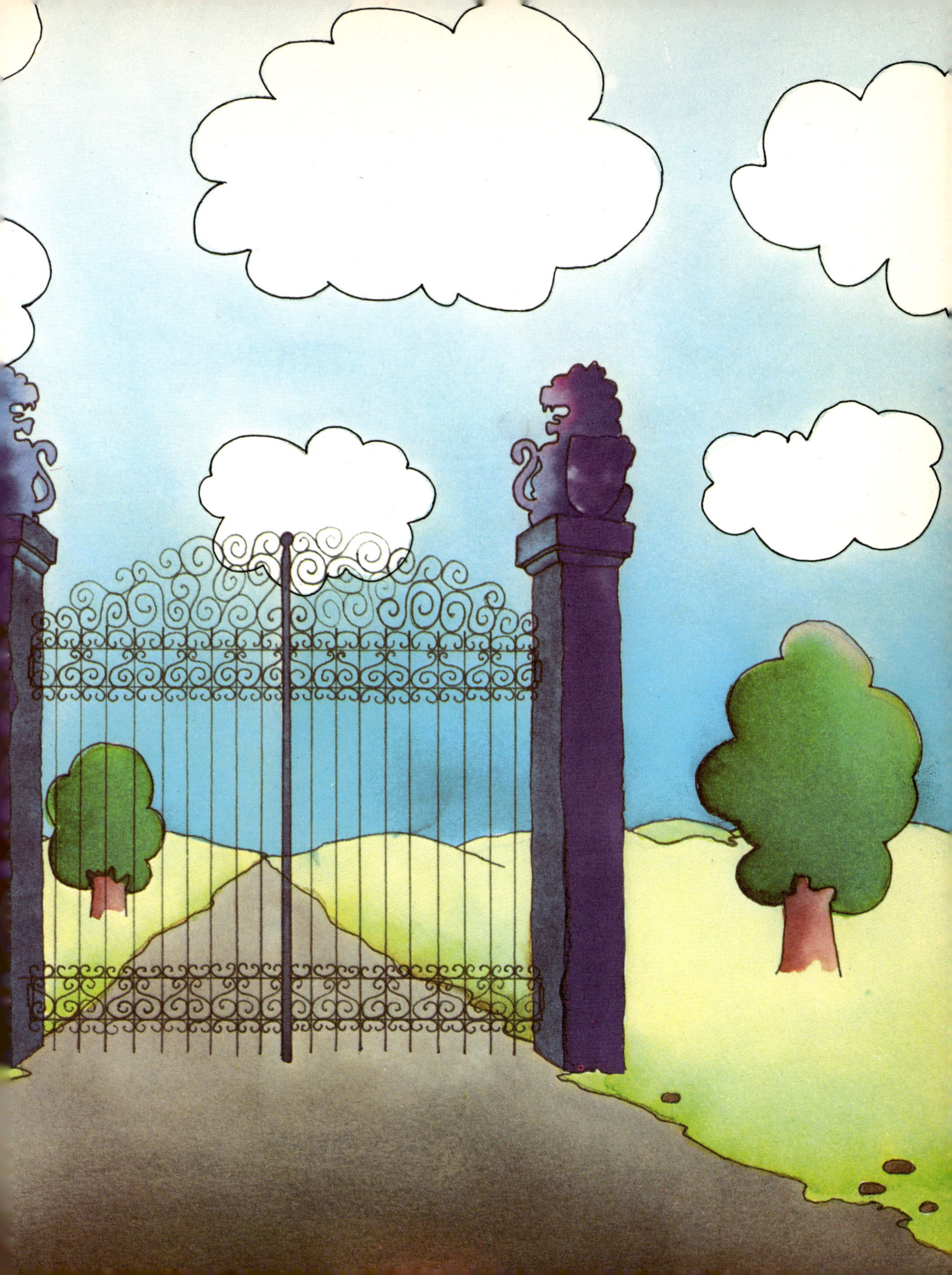

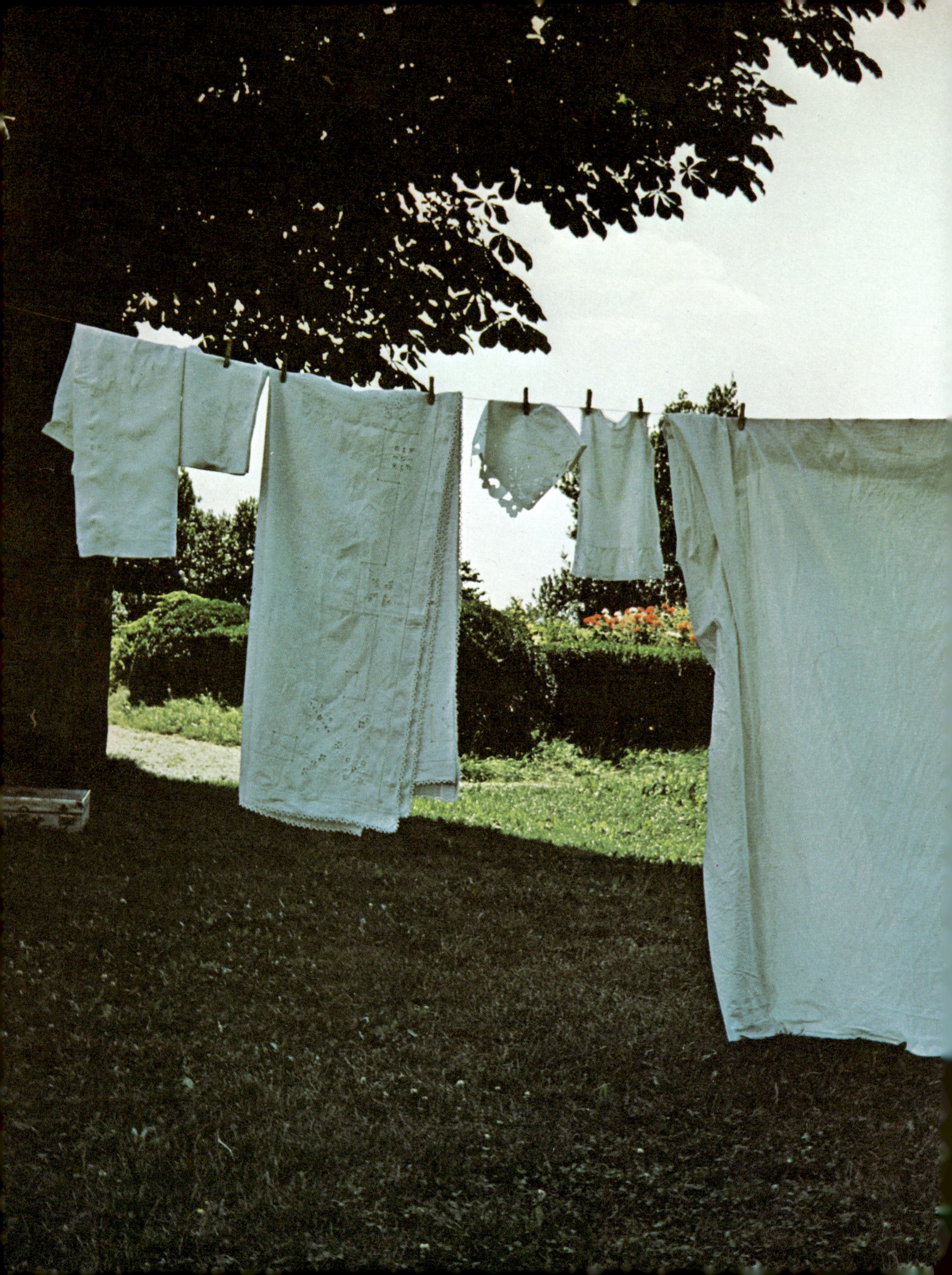

Washing on the line

The leisurely life of the French nobility and of the king and his court at the beautiful palace of Versailles was costing the country a lot of money. So were foreign wars and trade with overseas colonies. The king and his government had great difficulty collecting taxes from noblemen. So the burden of tax-paying fell on the middle and lower classes of people. Huge taxes were demanded to pay for France's expenses. People were angry about this, and many were made very poor. French thinkers and writers began to criticise the way things were going. Voltaire, one of the greatest French thinkers, began to write about what was wrong. The criticism which he and other thinkers made of France was like hanging their washing out for all the world to see. Now men knew that while the nobility had a rich way of life and sheets of lace, the common people were poor and had ragged sheets with holes.

Voltaire and other thinkers were very popular, even with the nobility. It became fashionable to criticize the evils of society. People seemed not to realize that popular criticism could lead to violent action. The poor became more and more determined to have a better way of life.

First moves

By the winter of 1787 things had gone from bad to worse in France. The king and his ministers in the government knew something had to be done. They tried to find new ways of raising more money, but they failed. Finally it was agreed that all three Estates in France would meet together.

The Estates General, a sort of national assembly, met in May 1789. The first moves of the assembled representatives of the French people were like a strange game of chess. Royalty (the black figures), the clergy (the blue figures), and nobles (the yellow figures) tried to keep an advantage over the Third Estate (the red figures) by refusing to give up their privileges.

Wigs thrown away

The French people were in a state of unrest over their unfair government. Many were starving because food crops had failed in the coldest winter for a century. When the Estates General met there was bitter argument about how to reform the kingdom. The king took little notice of either the national assembly's demands or of the serious rebellious attitude of his people.

The Third Estate (everyone except the nobility and the churchmen) met secretly in an indoor tennis court and declared themselves to be the true National Assembly of the French people. They agreed not to disband until they had prepared a constitution, (written laws) for France. This move frightened the noblemen, the clergy, and the king. The Third Estate had declared, in effect, that the people were the rightful rulers of the country.

Elegant white powdered wigs, worn by the nobility in the height of fashion, were suddenly no longer popular—they were a symbol of a hated class of men. Now some noblemen threw away their costly wigs and joined the Third Estate. Others were afraid and prepared to flee the country if necessary. The whole country was in a state of alarm and panic.

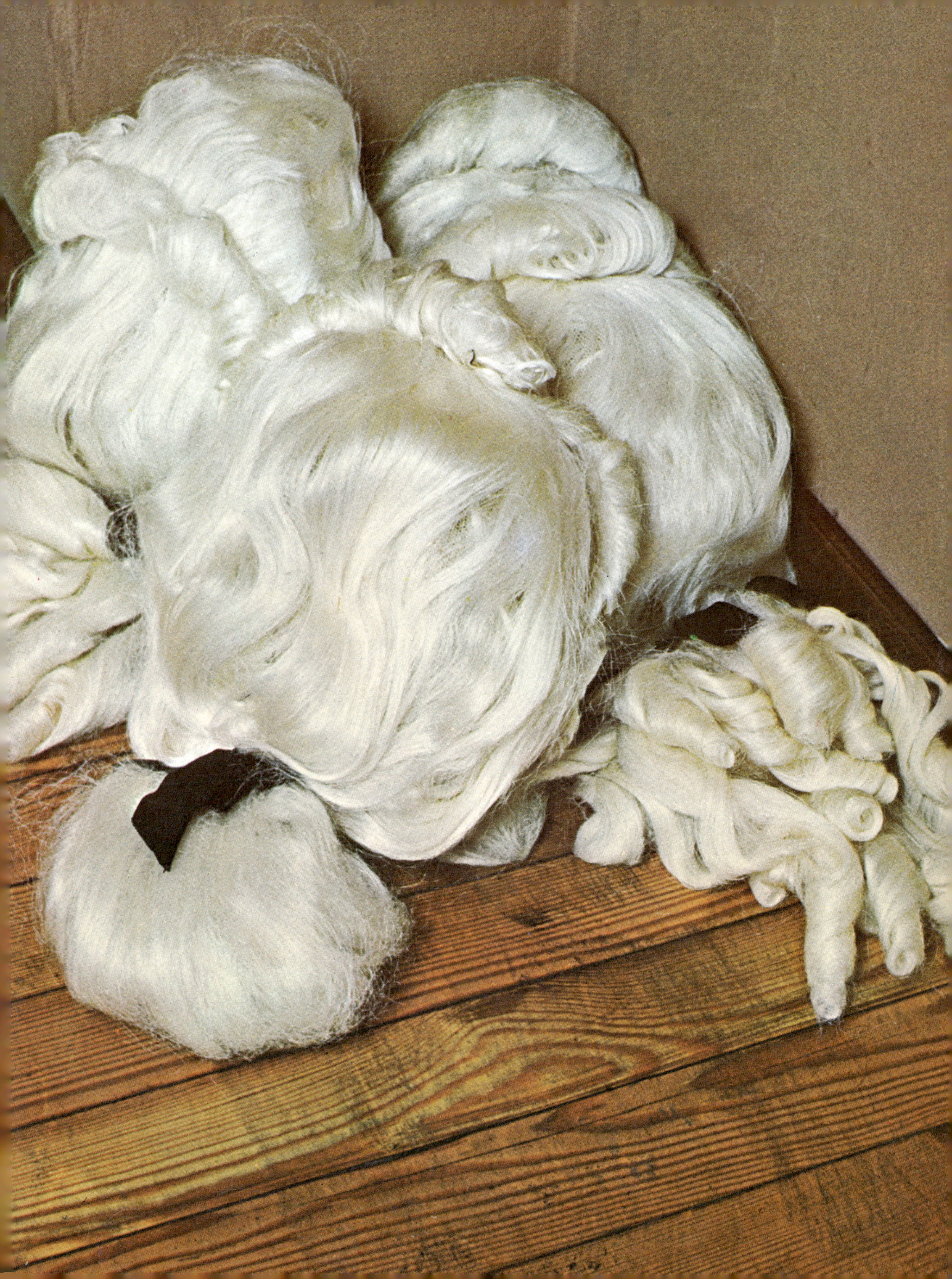

Breaking the symbol of power

In the earlier picture of the unusual chess game on pages 12–13, the two black figures stood for the French king and queen—the monarchy. In the year 1789 the Third Estate, now calling itself the National Assembly, held a meeting. At that meeting an event occurred which broke the power of the monarchy and set the French nation on a new path of government.

On 14th July, the people of Paris stormed the ancient fortress of the Bastille prison. Hunger, fear and panic had been widespread in France's capital city for several months. The Bastille was a symbol of all the injustices suffered by the people. Locked within its gates were starving men, women and children who had stolen bits of bread to survive. When the prison's walls were battered down and its guards murdered, the French Revolution had begun.

What Paris wants, France will have

The people of Paris, like all French people, were tired of the years of suffering and starving. They did not trust the king or the nobility. When King Louis XVI heard the news of the fall of the Bastille to the Paris mob, he said, "This is a great revolt." A courtier replied, "No, sir, it is a great revolution."

   The National Assembly understood that Paris, the capital, was determined that the whole country should be reformed. As a result, on 27th August it produced the famous *Declaration of the Rights of Man*, a kind of preamble (introduction), to the first constitution of France. Liberty (freedom), fraternity (brotherhood), and equality were now declared to be the rights of every French citizen. Frenchmen now believed that these natural rights would spill forth across the land to cure it of all its sicknesses.

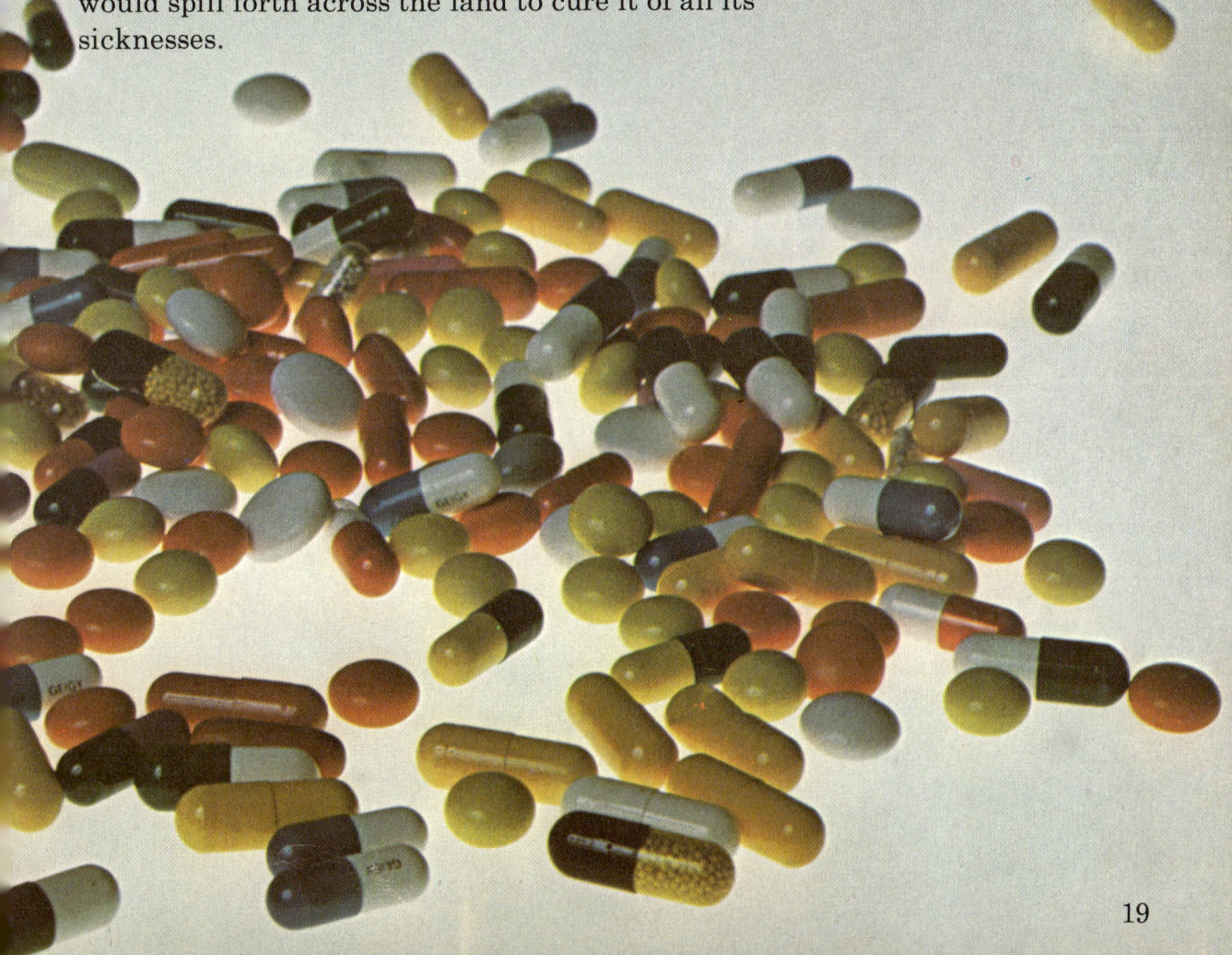

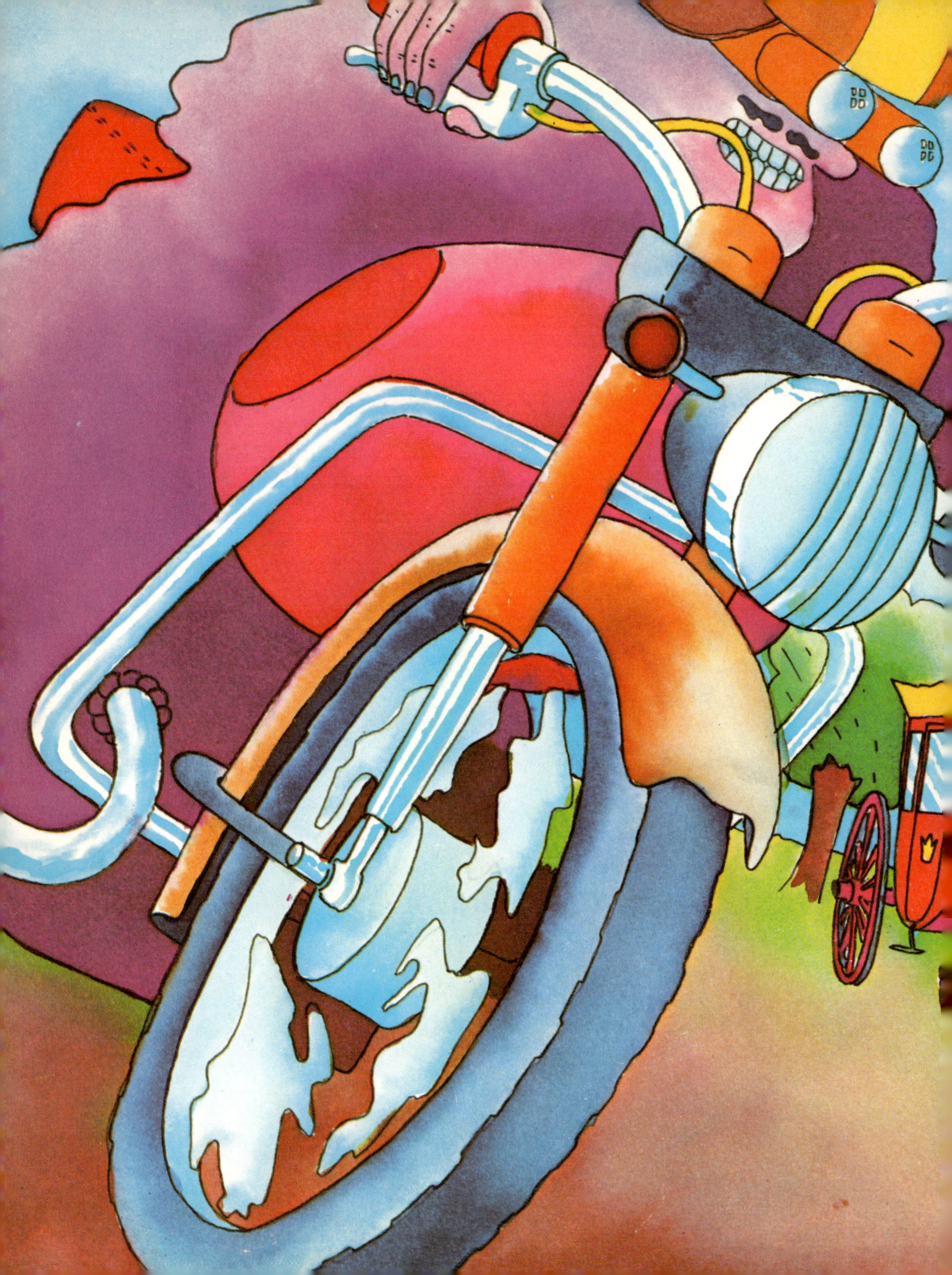

The people feel power

From the storming of the Bastille and on through the years of the French Revolution, the people changed as much of the old ways of doing things as they could. At one time they had lived blindly from day to day, never questioning whether they should have more freedom and a better life. Now they took the power that had been the privilege of the noble class, the Second Estate, into their own hands. They could almost touch their new power, and their new privileges, or rights. It was as if people who had once slowly dragged a nobleman's coach across the countryside, suddenly jumped onto a powerful motorcycle and felt the power of the engine as they whizzed forward on a new, exciting journey.

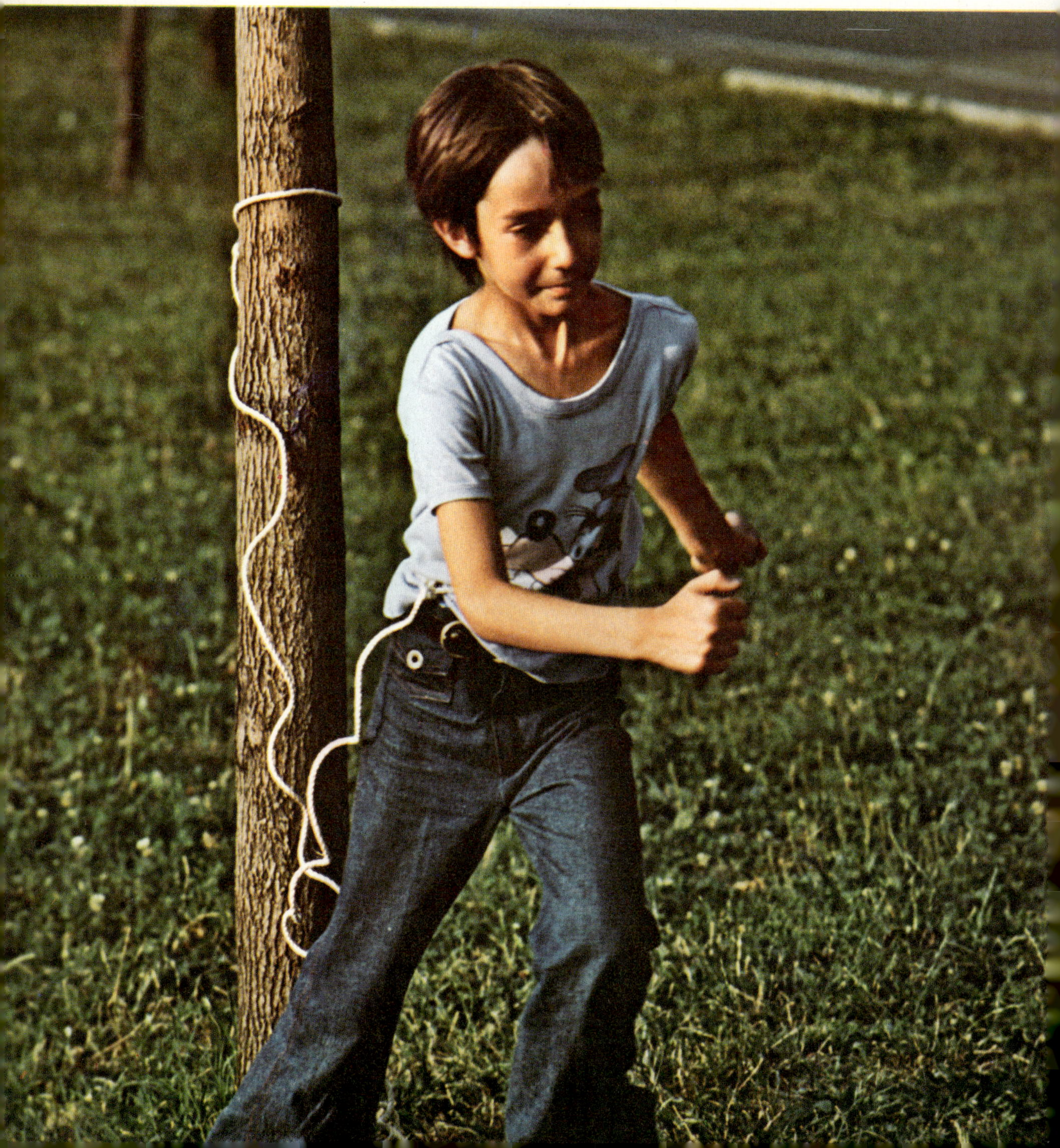

Restricting privilege

Once the French people began to feel their new power, they took matters into their own hands. They burned the houses of noblemen, and forced them to flee for their lives. The people were very suspicious of the king, and they captured him and forced him to live in the Tuileries palace in Paris. Here they could keep watch over him to make sure he was not seeking help from foreigners to overthrow the revolution.

The Paris mobs and rioting peasants were led on by members of the middle classes, called the bourgeoisie in France. Although the Third Estate was made up of all classes of people who were not royal, noble, or clergymen, the leaders of the Third Estate were bankers, lawyers, businessmen, tradesmen, craftsmen, and thinkers and scholars. Many were young, hot-headed, and wild with the new ideas of liberty and equality. The Third Estate kept constant watch over the First and Second Estates, exactly as if they had tied their enemies to a tree with just enough rope to move about a little bit, but not enough to allow them to escape. Members of the First and Second Estates fled from France whenever they could. They were terrified of the new citizens who had become brutal and ruthless in restricting the privileges of the old powerful classes.

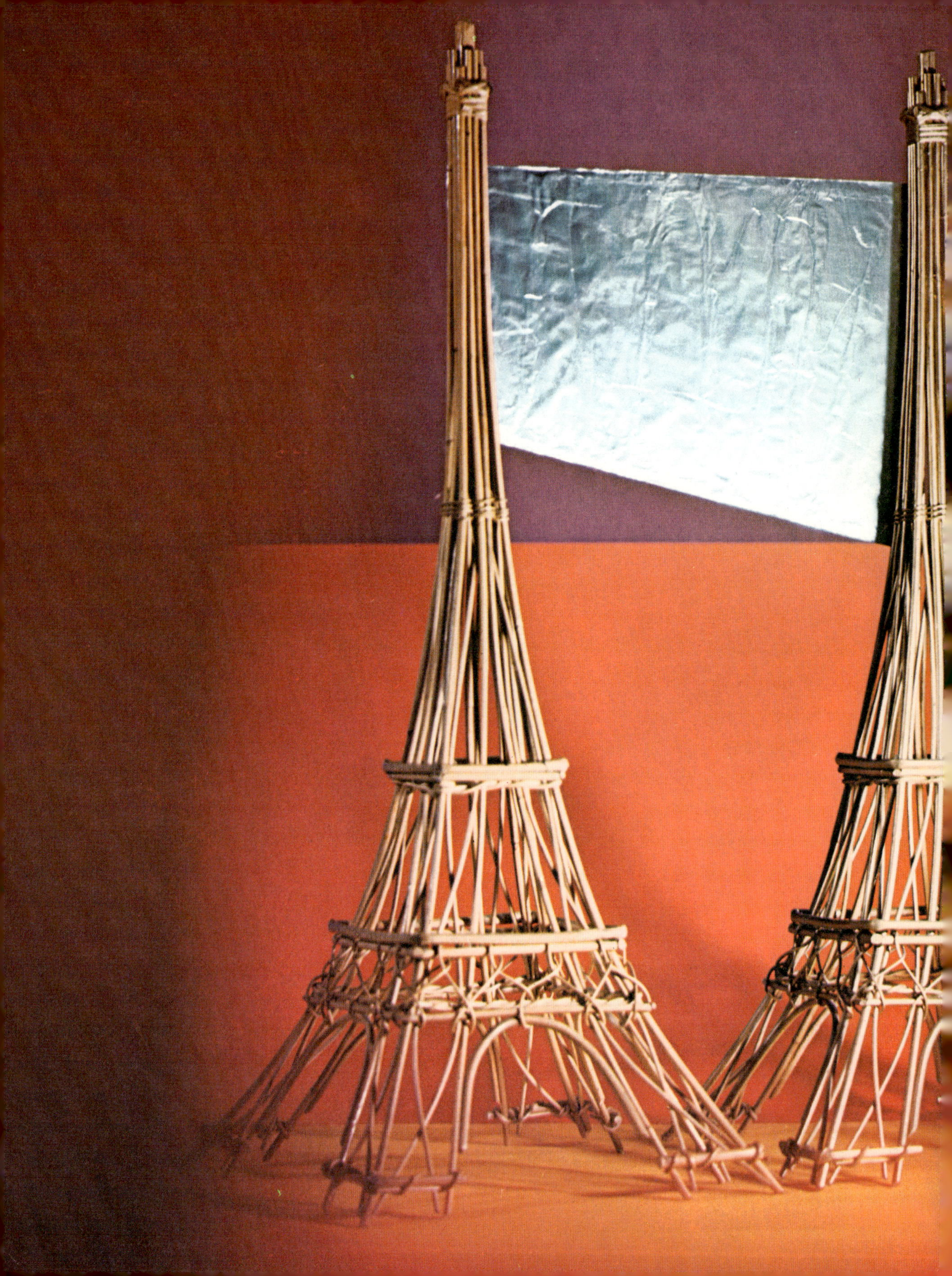

The days of terror

The picture shows two Eiffel towers, with a large tinfoil knife blade stretched between them. The Eiffel Tower was not built until 1889, but ever since it has symbolized the beautiful city of Paris. The tinfoil knife symbolizes the guillotine— the horrible weapon with which enemies of the Revolution had their heads cut off.

   The French Revolution was an exciting turning point in the search for liberty by Europeans. The glory of the Revolution is often forgotten because of the horrible bloodshed that took place while it was happening. Many people were sent to their death as enthusiastic Paris mobs cheered, simply because they were suspected of being sympathizers with the nobility. Even the king and queen were guillotined in the excitement of revolution. The people always feared that their liberty and equality would be taken from them, and acts of violence became commonplace. The time when no one felt safe was known as the Reign of Terror. By 1794 the days of terror were coming to an end. Paris and all of France had had enough bloodshed. France was also engaged in wars throughout Europe with countries which were thought to be enemies of the Revolution. The French people needed a period of calm. They needed to feel safe once more.

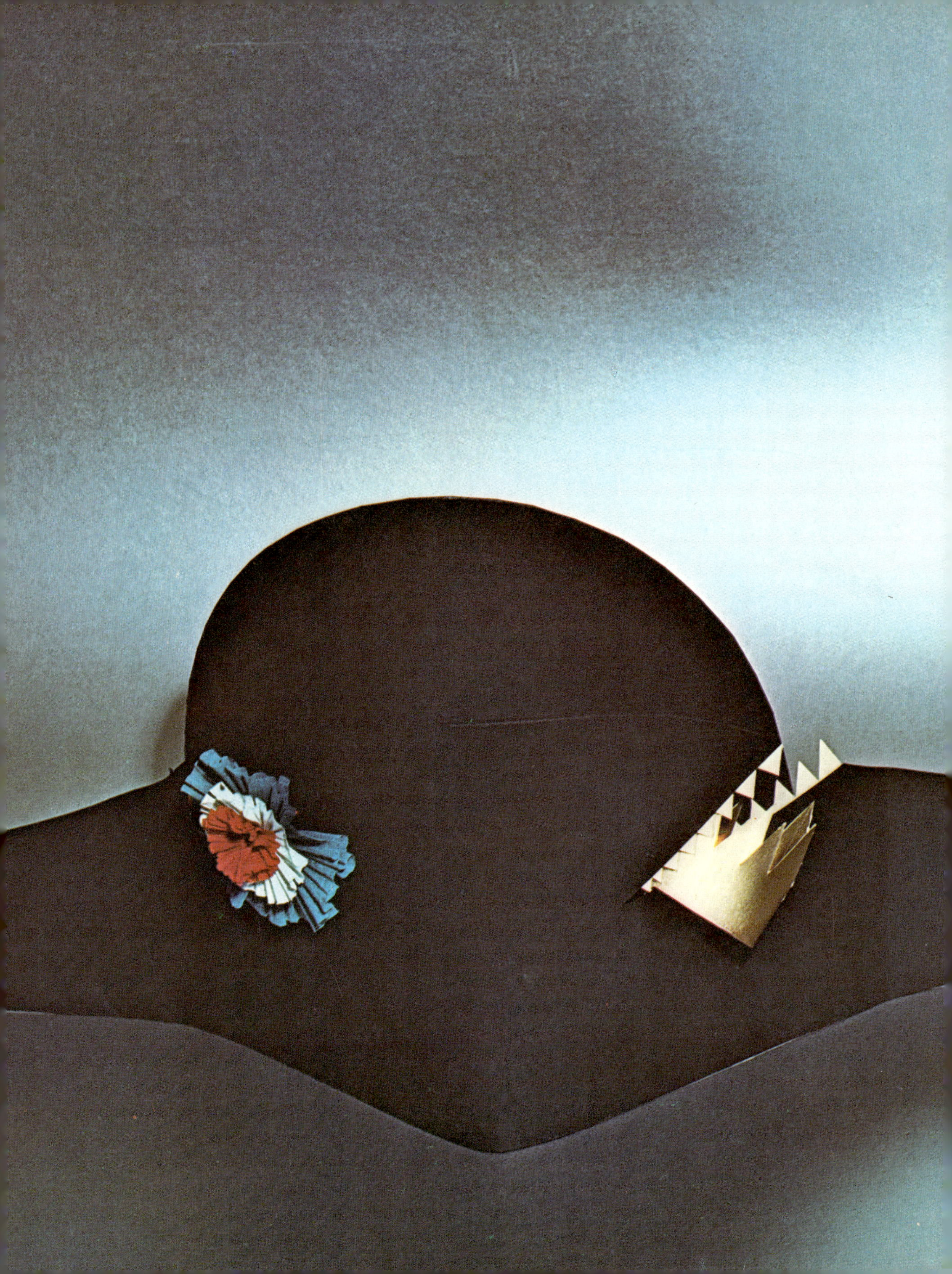

From citizen to emperor

Napoleon Bonaparte was born in 1769 in the city of Ajaccio on the island of Corsica. He is known to history as the "man of destiny"; he was a man destined to change the course of history in Europe.

As a young man he was trained in a military school. There he dreamed that Corsica might one day gain its freedom from French rule.

In 1789 the French Revolution broke out, and four years later France was at war with Britain. Napoleon was a clever young military commander; he forced the British out of the port of Toulon. In 1795 he helped the new government, the Directory, to come to power in France. Under the Directory all men were simply French citizens and supposed to be equal. From this time on Citizen Bonaparte began to command French armies and win brilliant victories. He had taken the first few steps on the path from citizen to emperor of the French.

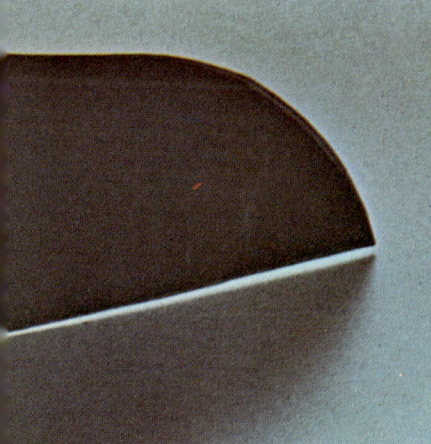

A hen looking after her brood

Napoleon fought and won battles for France in many far off lands. He campaigned in Egypt and in the Middle East. He returned to France secretly in 1799 and became First Consul. He cared very much for the welfare of France, but he was also ambitious for power for himself. The French people were glad to have him in command of events. They felt safe with such a great soldier. They had been fighting wars and were frightened by the past horrors of the revolution. Now they had a master who would look after them as a mother hen fiercely protects her young.

Napoleon defeated the Austrians in two major battles and in 1801 the two countries signed a peace treaty. All of Europe was amazed at the strength of Napoleon's armies. In the next year, France and Britain talked peace, but soon they were at war again.

For five years Napoleon supported the ordinary French people and upheld the ideals of the revolution: liberty, fraternity and equality. By 1804 he was so powerful that he declared himself Emperor of the French and crowned himself with a wreath of golden laurel. After his coronation, he surrounded himself with a court. So Citizen Bonaparte was now a ruler like an all powerful king. He was no longer an ordinary citizen and few dared to oppose him.

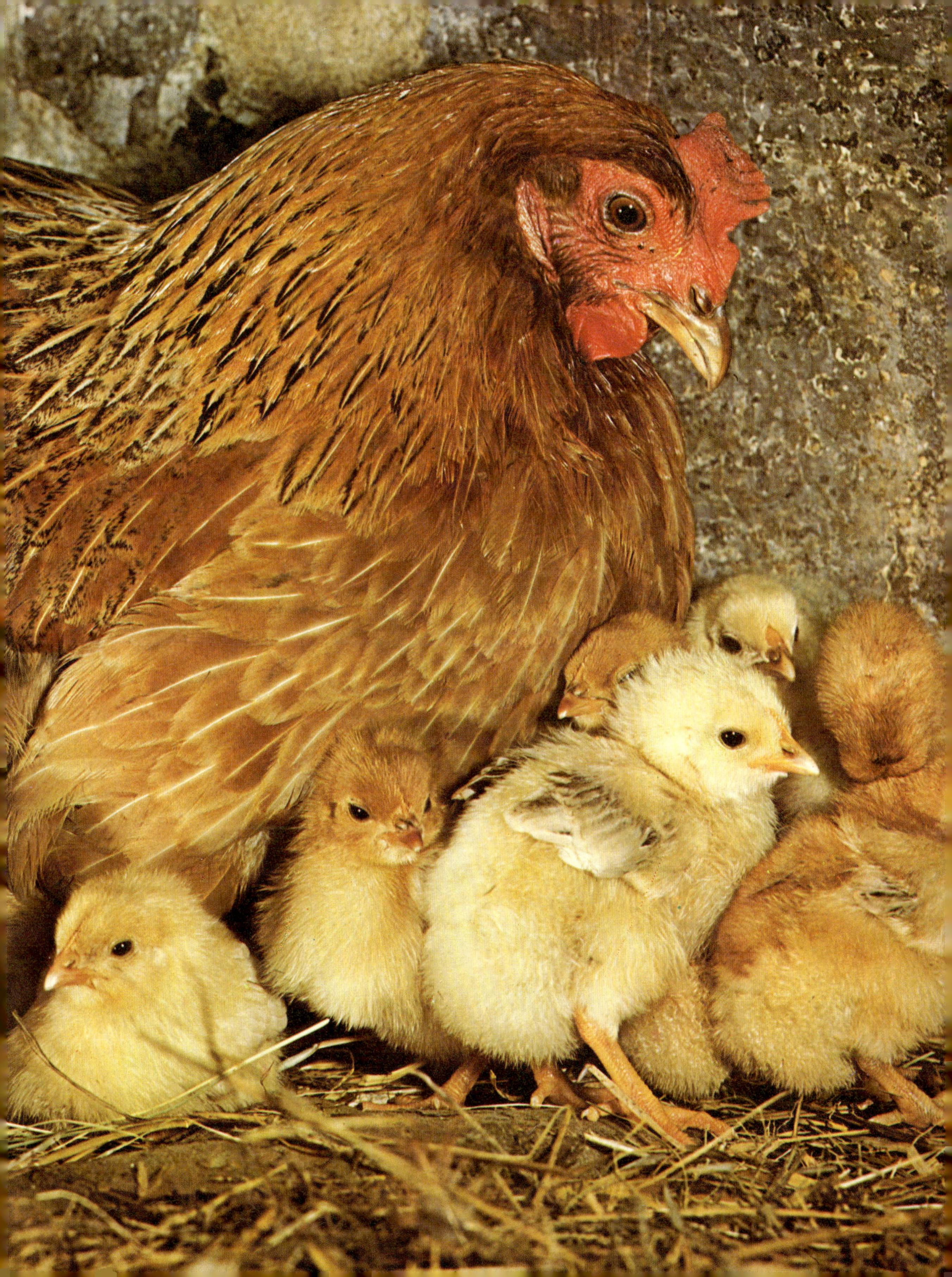

The brilliant general

Napoleon was a brilliant general.

He had a brain that was lightning quick. When events took an unexpected turn in the course of a battle, he was ready with a new plan. While his enemies stuck rigidly to their battle plans, and suffered for it, Napoleon took them by surprise over and over again. The picture shows a white horse—which Napoleon always liked to ride—with a small computer in the saddle.

Napoleon had such a good memory and the ability to study and remember so many facts that if he were alive today men might compare him to a computer.

Napoleon's armies were well trained and well equipped. He made good use of his men, his artillery (guns and cannons), and his cavalry (soldiers on horseback). He told his soldier officers exactly what he expected them to do throughout a battle. He had spies who gathered as much information as they could about what the enemy intended to do in a battle. If there was a weakness in his battle plans, Napoleon wanted to know about it in advance so that he could correct it. Because he planned every detail, Napoleon was able to see that his armies carried out attacks speedily and gained good advantages.

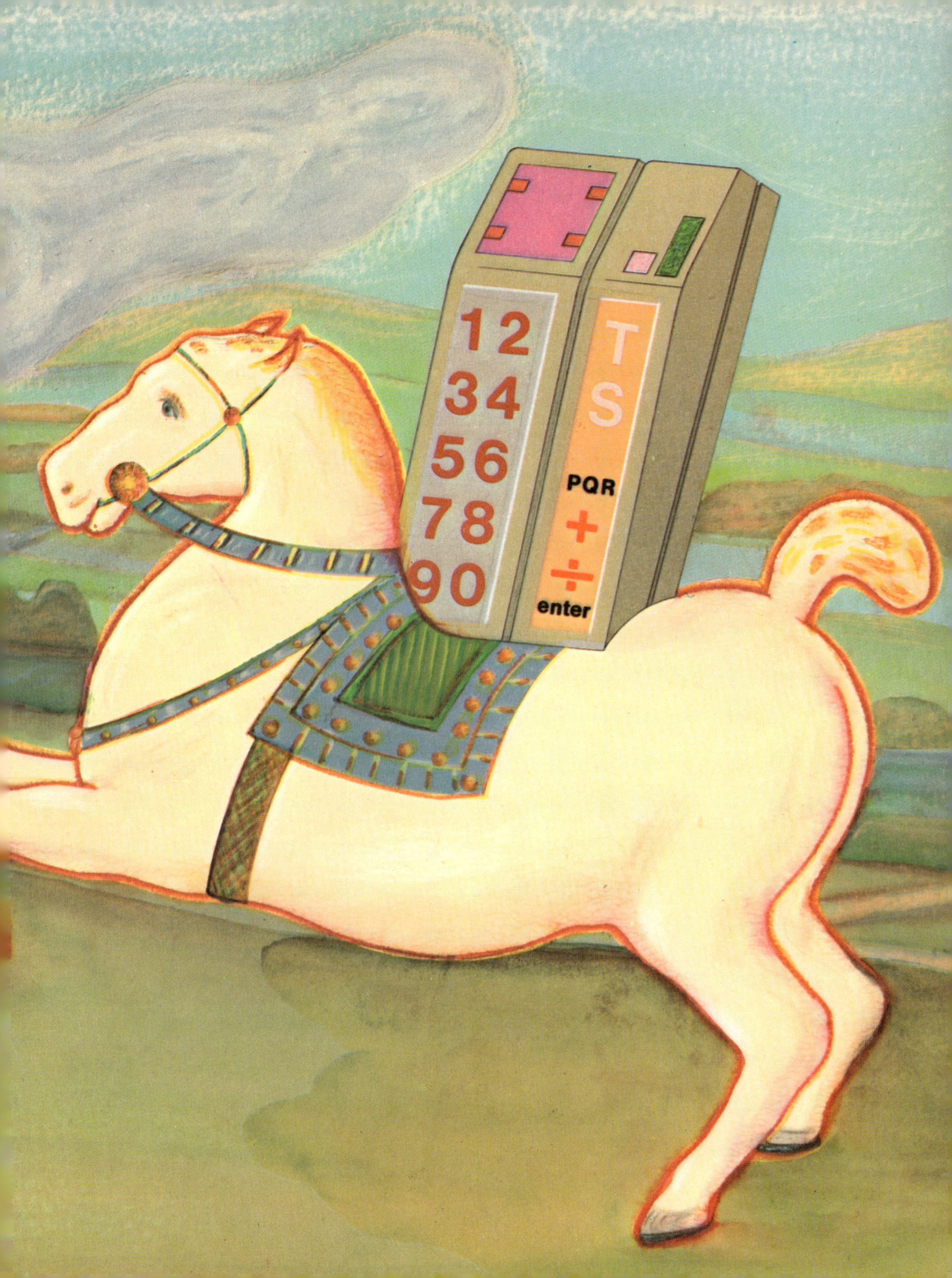
12
34
56
78
90
T
S
PQR
+
÷
enter

Cutting Britain off

Napoleon never understood sea power, as he understood military power on land. Viscount Horatio Nelson, Britain's famous sea lord, beat the French and Spanish navies off Cape Trafalgar in 1805. He lost his life, but helped limit French power.

Napoleon ordered Europe to blockade British shipping, that is to stop them reaching port to trade. So Britain in turn blockaded European coastlines and grabbed the ships of the Danish navy. Napoleon had tried to cut off tiny Britain from her rich sea trade, but Britain held out. She also began to seize the European colonies and possessions overseas. She supported the enemies of Napoleon and slowly increased her power.

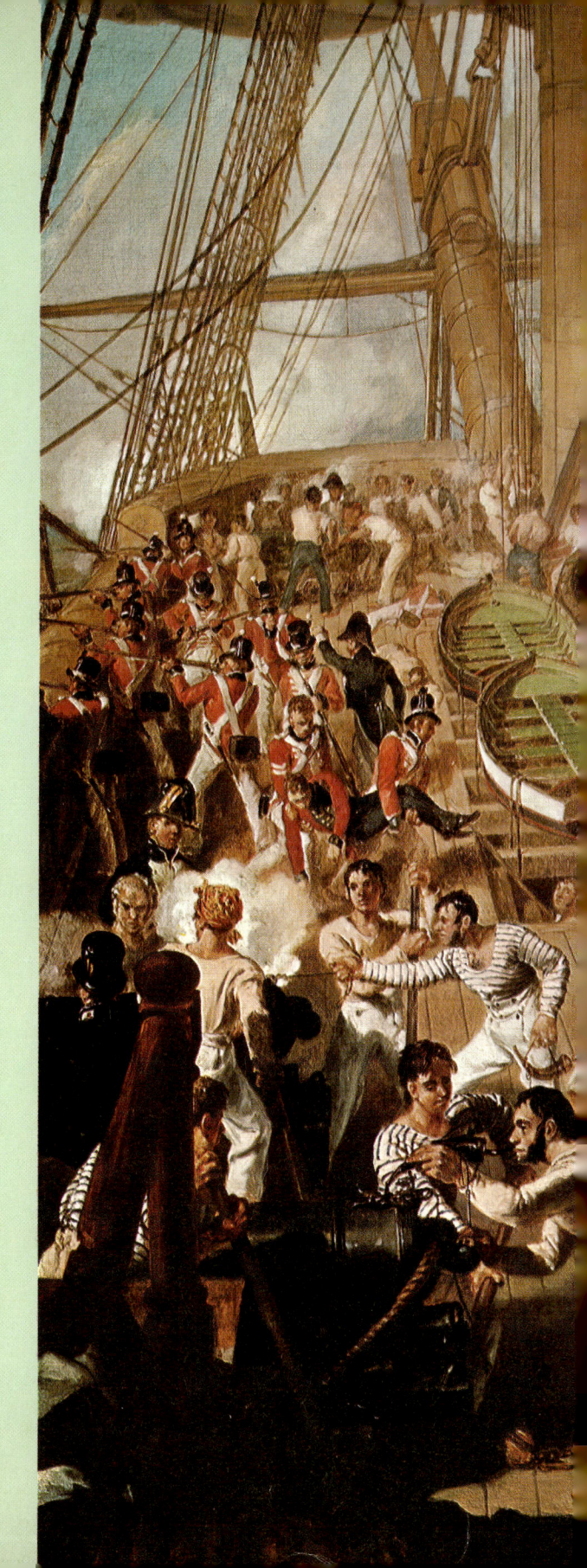

Photograph: The National Maritime Museum

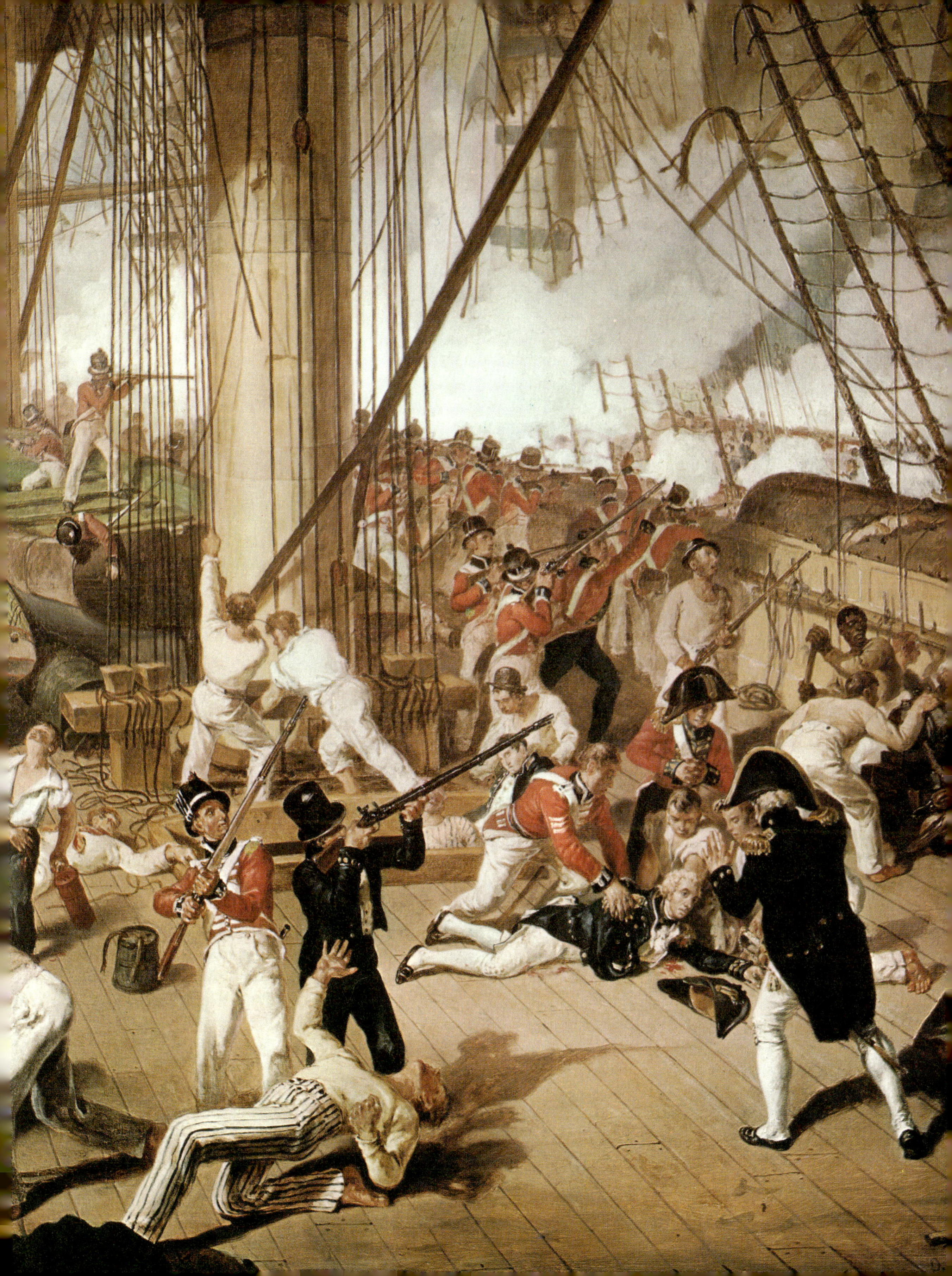

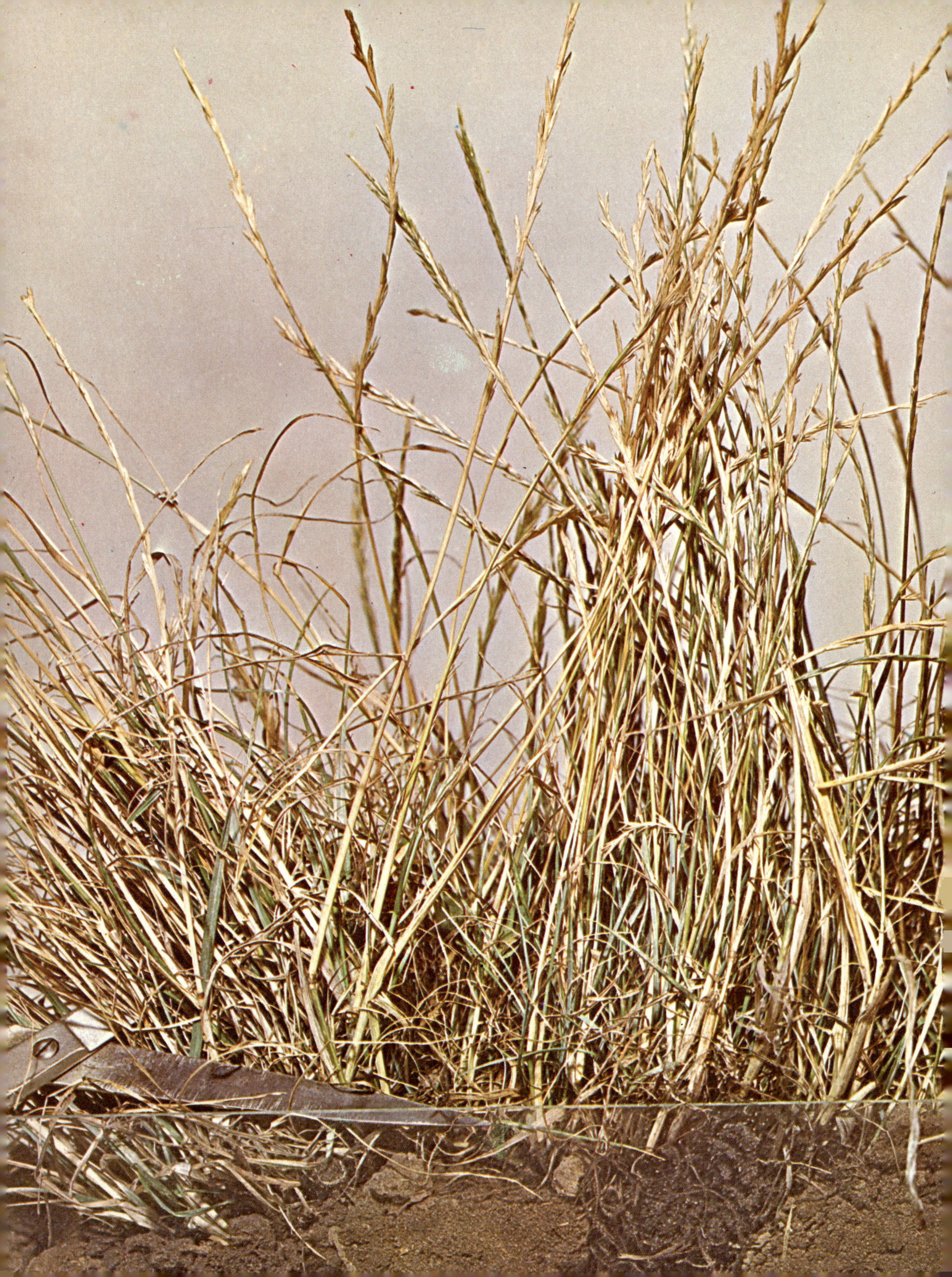

Shearing grass

Napoleon's army was sweeping across Europe cutting down his enemies almost as easily as a pair of sharp shears cut through grass. The French democracy became the Napoleonic Empire. Except for Britain, all Europe stood in fear of the unbeatable French.

Defeat at last

But defeat for Napoleon's Grand Army came in the winter of 1812. The brave general believed his intention of freeing the peasants and improving their lives would make him welcome. Instead as he pushed forward the

Russians retreated, burning the land behind them so that there was no food or shelter for the French soldiers.

Napoleon reached Moscow but an early winter set in that year, and thousands of the French soldiers died in the bitter cold. Like the sticks standing on their white paint background, Napoleon's soldiers showed up clearly against the icy wasteland of Russia. Stranded and alone, without food or shelter in the vast Russian wasteland, they died in their thousands. The Grand Army's retreat from Russia was even worse. The bitterness of Russia's winter had defeated Napoleon.

Power and glory left behind

In Russia Napoleon lost great numbers of his soldiers—not only Frenchmen, but soldiers from Germany, Italy, Portugal, Spain and Holland.

The Grand Army was shattered. Napoleon left his army and hurried back to Paris to beg for more men and supplies. But when Napoleon's allies heard of his retreat they no longer supported him. Prussia, the most powerful state of Germany, joined with Russia against him. Austria declared war on him. So did Sweden. Napoleon fought some desperate battles, but he and his troops were pushed back into France.

By April of 1814 he was forced to give up his power in favour of Louis XVIII. Napoleon had to leave behind him all the symbols of his power and his glory. He was sent into exile on the island of Elba.

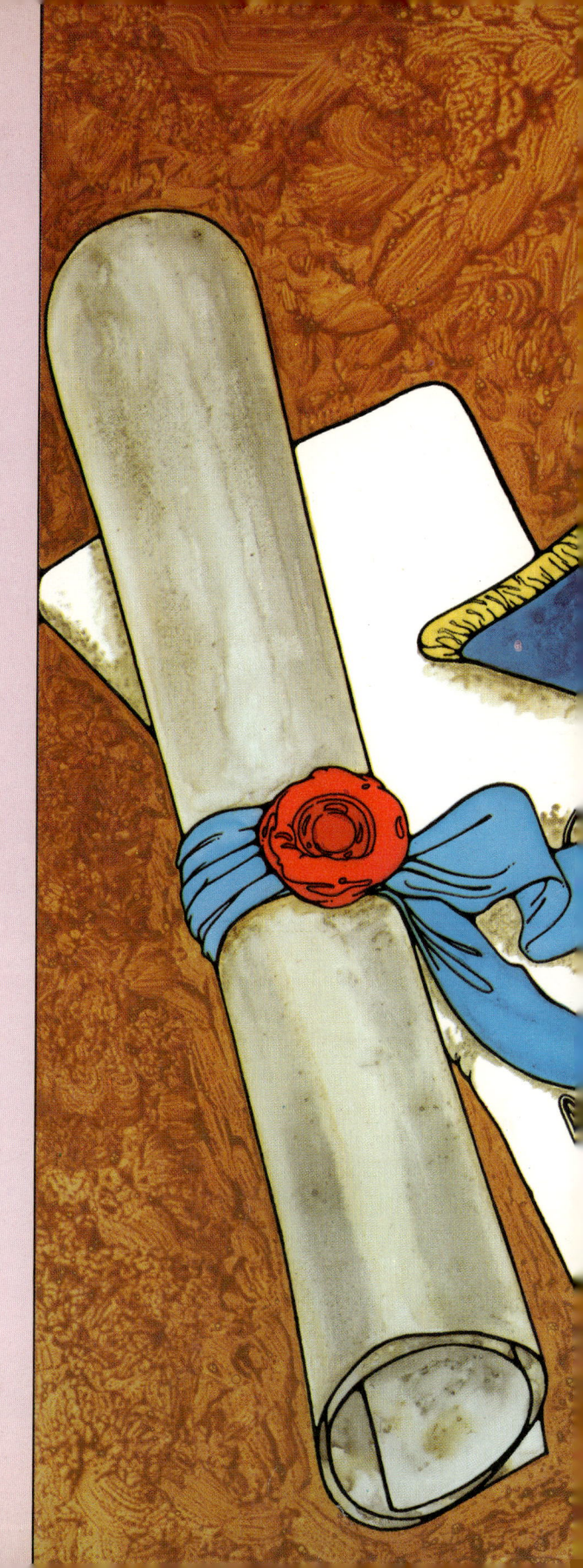

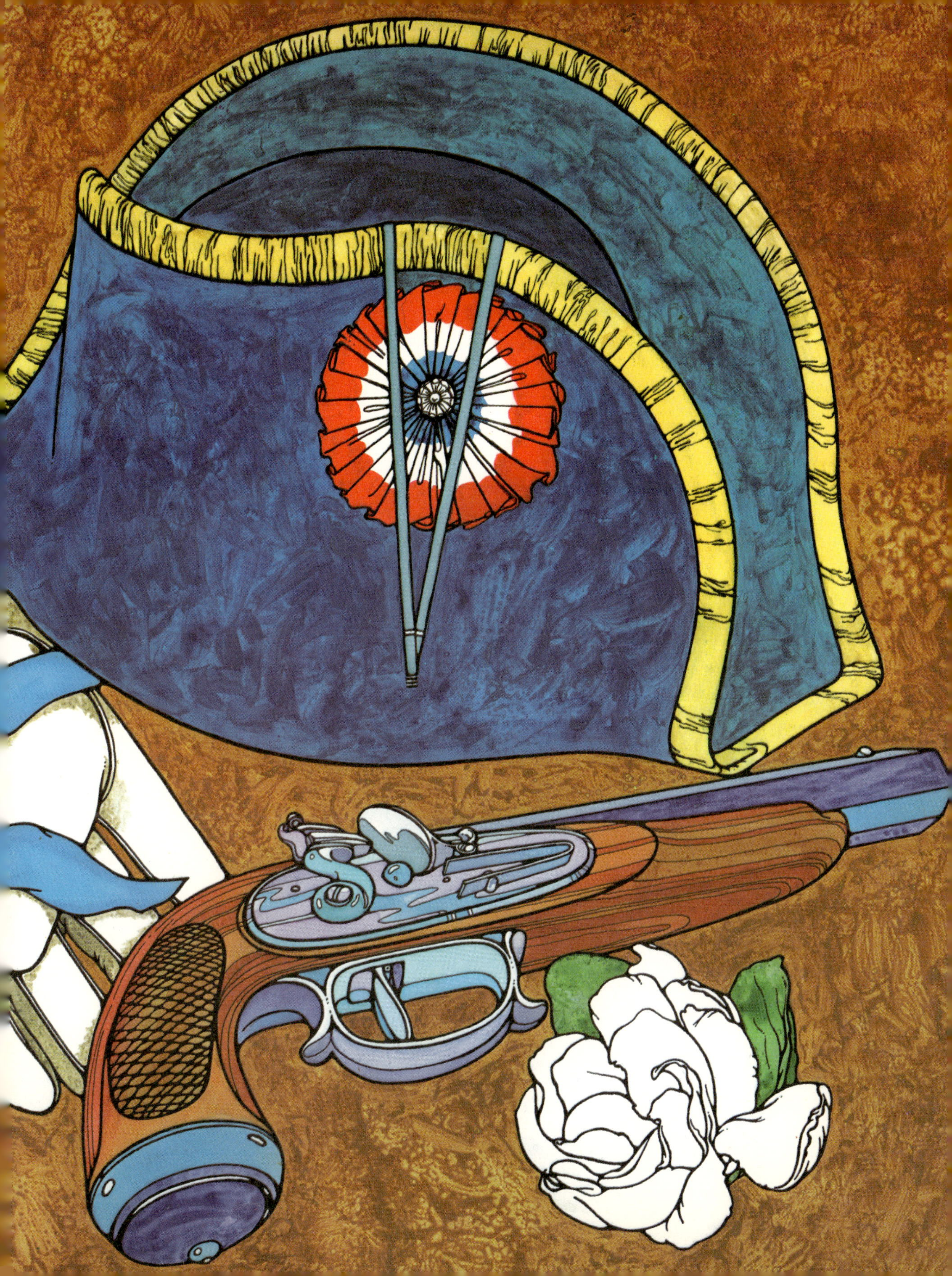

The final defeat

Within a year of his exile, Napoleon was back in France. Many French soldiers joined him, and King Louis fled from Paris. Napoleon proposed peace plans, but the powers of Europe did not trust him, and rose against him. Napoleon marched his troops into Belgium, but he no longer planned his battles so well. The French army met the British army at Waterloo—Napoleon faced the Duke of Wellington. In a brilliant campaign, the French were soundly defeated. Napoleon surrendered. He was banished to the island of St Helena in the southern Atlantic Ocean. There he lived with a collection of items from his past life—military weapons, and personal mementoes.

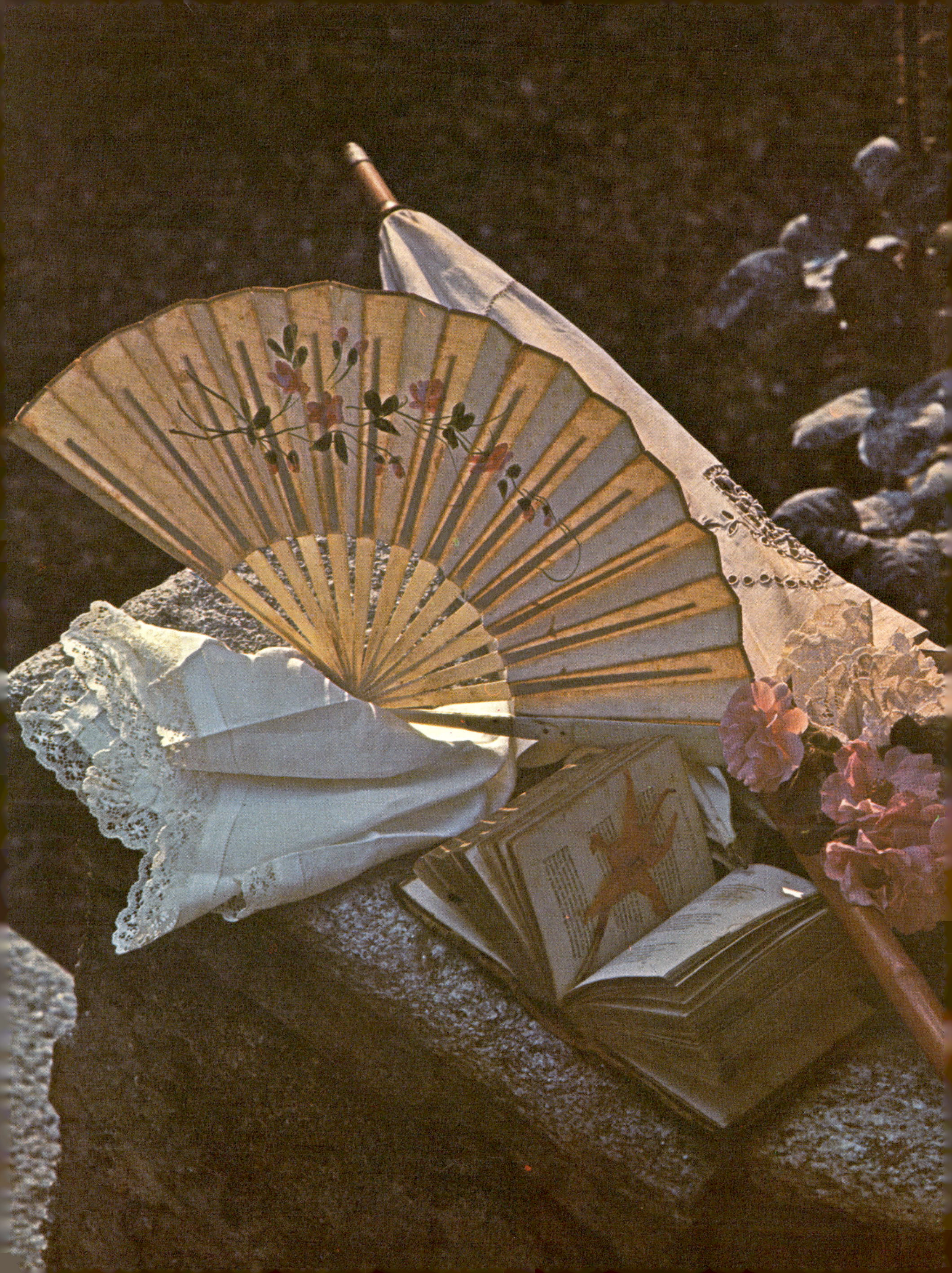

A New Age Begins

Peace and order

Europe breathed a sigh of relief when Napoleon's career was truly ended. But the monarchs and the statesmen of Europe now had to face new problems.

Rather than keep on trying to gain power over each other, they began to worry more about their own countries and how their own people lived. Everywhere people began to think more about the problems of living. They studied these problems and discussed them. In France, Britain, Holland, and most of the countries of Europe, men read, thought and discussed the governing of their countries, and of how people could best live and work together.

Cobwebs on crowns

By the beginning of the nineteenth century, people in most countries began to have new ideas about how they should be ruled or governed. The crowns on the heads of European rulers had got dusty with cobwebs. The cobwebs were all the old ideas about how kings, queens, princes and dukes should rule their people. Some rulers thought their crowns had lost a bit of their shine over the centuries too. Spiders' webs of ideas about a ruler's divine right to rule needed to be swept clean away.

The best way to get rid of the cobwebs and to polish up a crown is to gain the people's respect and approval. Men and women now wanted rulers to recognize their natural rights. A ruler's subjects wanted to have their natural rights written down as laws. Such laws are called a constitution. A ruler who ruled by a fair and just set of laws would probably keep his crown on his head. The British were ruled by a king and a constitution. Other Europeans wanted the same kind of fair rule. People no longer believed that a ruler could do just as he pleased without their consent.

Patching up the leaks

After Napoleon's wars, Austria, Prussia (the largest of the German states), Russia, and Great Britain met at Vienna in 1814. This meeting, called the Congress of Vienna, began to restore the rulers of the European countries. Putting the old kind of rulers back into power was a bit like trying to patch up a leaking garden hose. Europe was changing, but the powerful countries were determined to hold back the change for as long as possible. By 1815 some of the members of the Congress signed an agreement called the Holy Alliance. The alliance drew up a map of Europe, with borders for each state and country. The man behind the agreement was Prince Metternich of Austria. He knew Europe was worn out with war and revolution. He used the alliance to make sure no revolutions or wars were started in or between the countries which signed the agreement. For almost forty years, the patched up Europe remained calm. But slowly the people began to demand more freedom and to question their rulers' right to govern. Then the patches in the old garden hose began to give way, first here and then there.

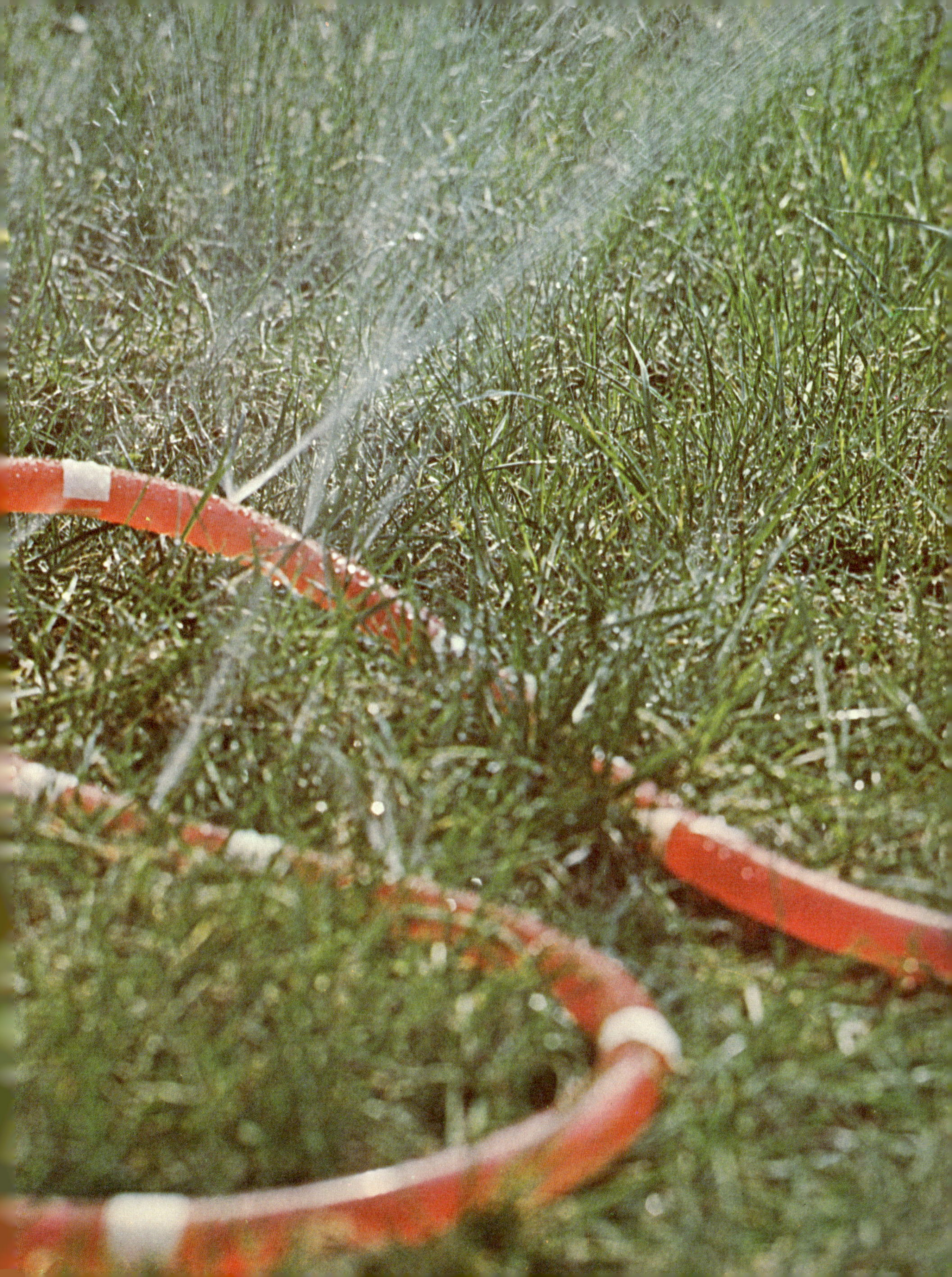

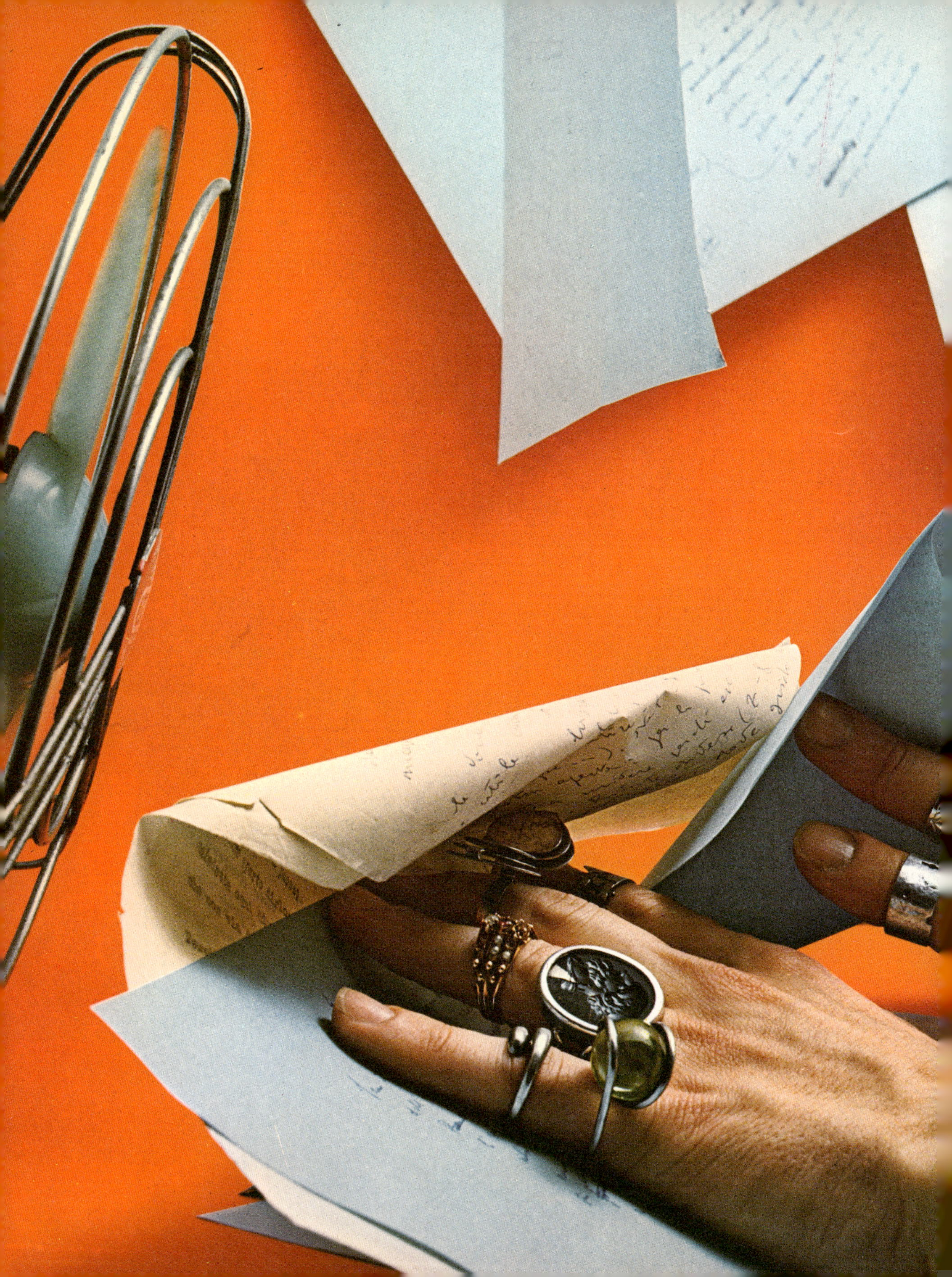

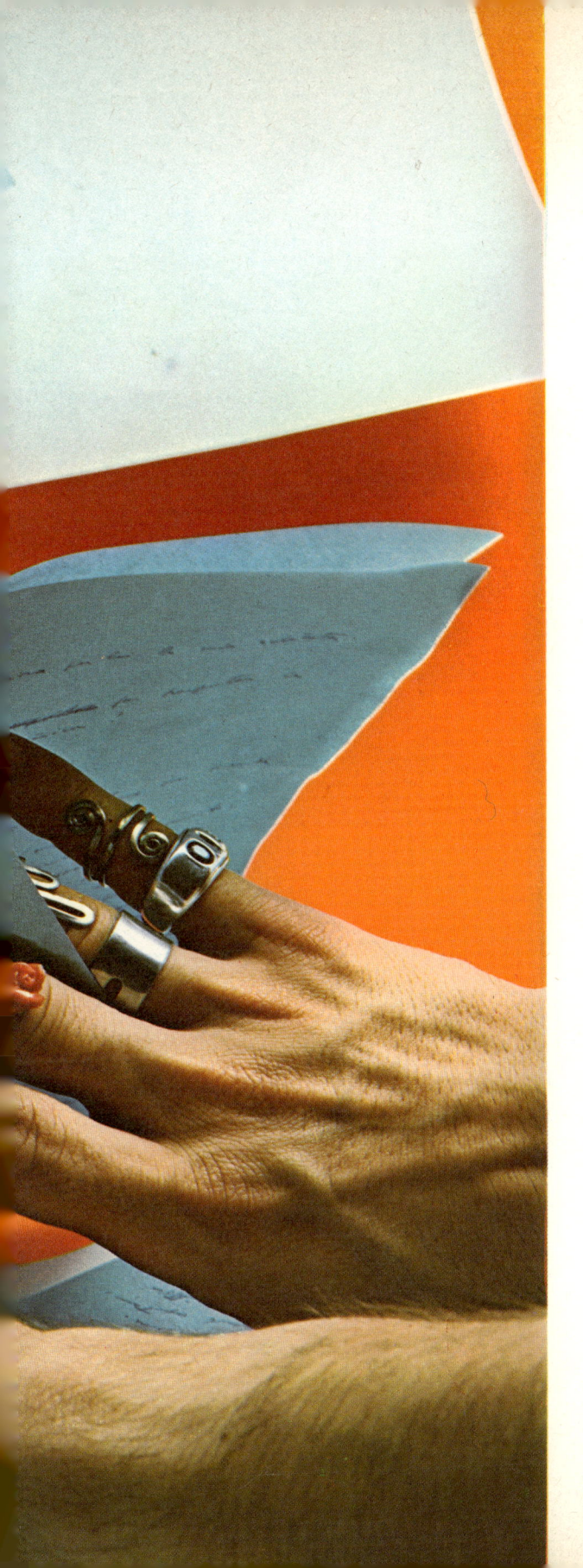

Ideas in the wind

In countries where people were free to speak and write about their ideas, new thoughts spread quickly. Where people were not so free, secret societies were often formed. They worked and planned for a better or fairer form of government. The societies acted like a small fan stirring the air. New ideas, freer ideas, were like a breath of fresh air to people who were ruled by divine right rather than by their consent.

In Germany, young students formed such secret societies. One was called the Universal German Student Society. Because the society was secret, members had to know how to recognize each other. They had secret code writing or perhaps special emblems which only members would recognize. One of the society's leaders believed in keeping physically fit. So gymnasiums were opened where students could study and perform sports. Prince Metternich had spies in the gymnasiums. He and the German leaders knew about the secret student meetings from spies. One spy was killed when the students discovered him, and so Metternich closed down the gymnasiums. The Prince thought the secret society was dangerous to peace because the students wanted less stern rule by the government. He tried to stop the tide of protest and change.

Chopping up the old powers

The old order of ruling had mostly been restored at the Congress of Vienna. To the ordinary people it seemed that nothing had changed. Soon they grew restless and slowly power changed hands. The middle class gained more power. As the working class saw this, they too wanted more say in the way their lives were governed. It made very little difference to people whether they were ruled by kings or by people with money. They worked long, hard hours, struggled to find enough food to feed their families, and found that what rights they had were ignored.

In the early nineteenth century, the desire for freedom first erupted far away from Europe. The United States had already obtained freedom from British rule. With this example, the people of South America rebelled against Spain and Portugal. José San Martin and Simon Bolivar became the great South American "liberators" or freedom fighters. Against great odds, the two men chopped up the Spanish and Portuguese powers.

The salad days were over for the old European colonial powers in South America. Salad days are the good times, when someone or something is young and fresh.

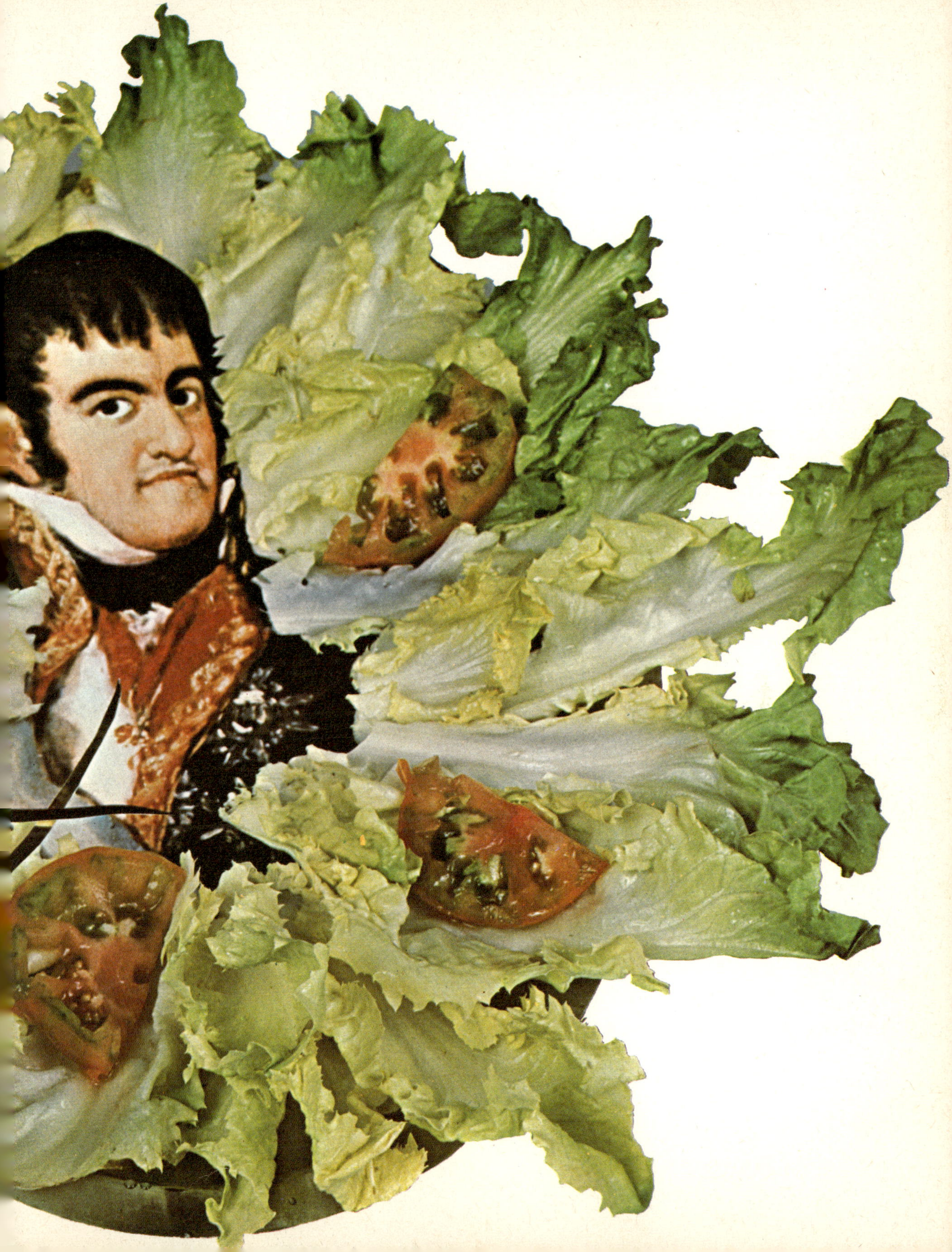

The citizen-king

In France after 1815, the king ruled with a parliament and was supposed to be responsible for his actions to the parliament. The men who elected the deputies or representatives to the French parliament had to be rich—so noblemen and richer businessmen were the only ones who could vote. The common people had little say in matters of government.

In 1830 Charles X ruled France. Charles believed that kings had the right to do whatever they wished, and in July 1830 he made a stupid and fatal mistake. He suspended the freedoms of the constitution of France and announced that he would rule by royal decree. Both the middle class and the workers were outraged. Riots broke out in Paris with fierce street fighting. As a result the crown of France was offered to the young Duke of Orleans, Louis-Phillipe, on the understanding that he would become a citizen-king. Louis-Phillipe wore the tri-colour emblem of liberty, fraternity and equality (red, white and blue) as well as the fleur-de-lis, the symbol of the French royal family. While Louis-Phillipe walked about Paris shaking hands with commoners, the middle class seized power. For the common citizens, the 1830 revolution was not exactly a great success.

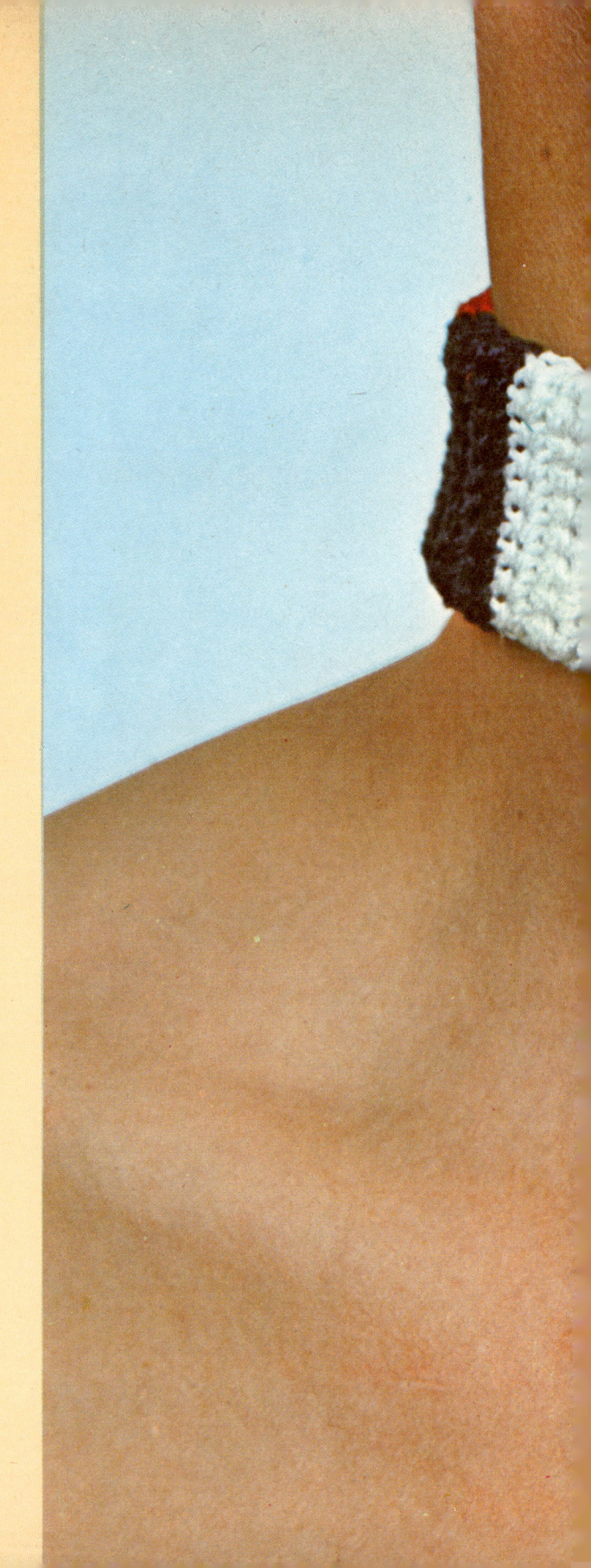

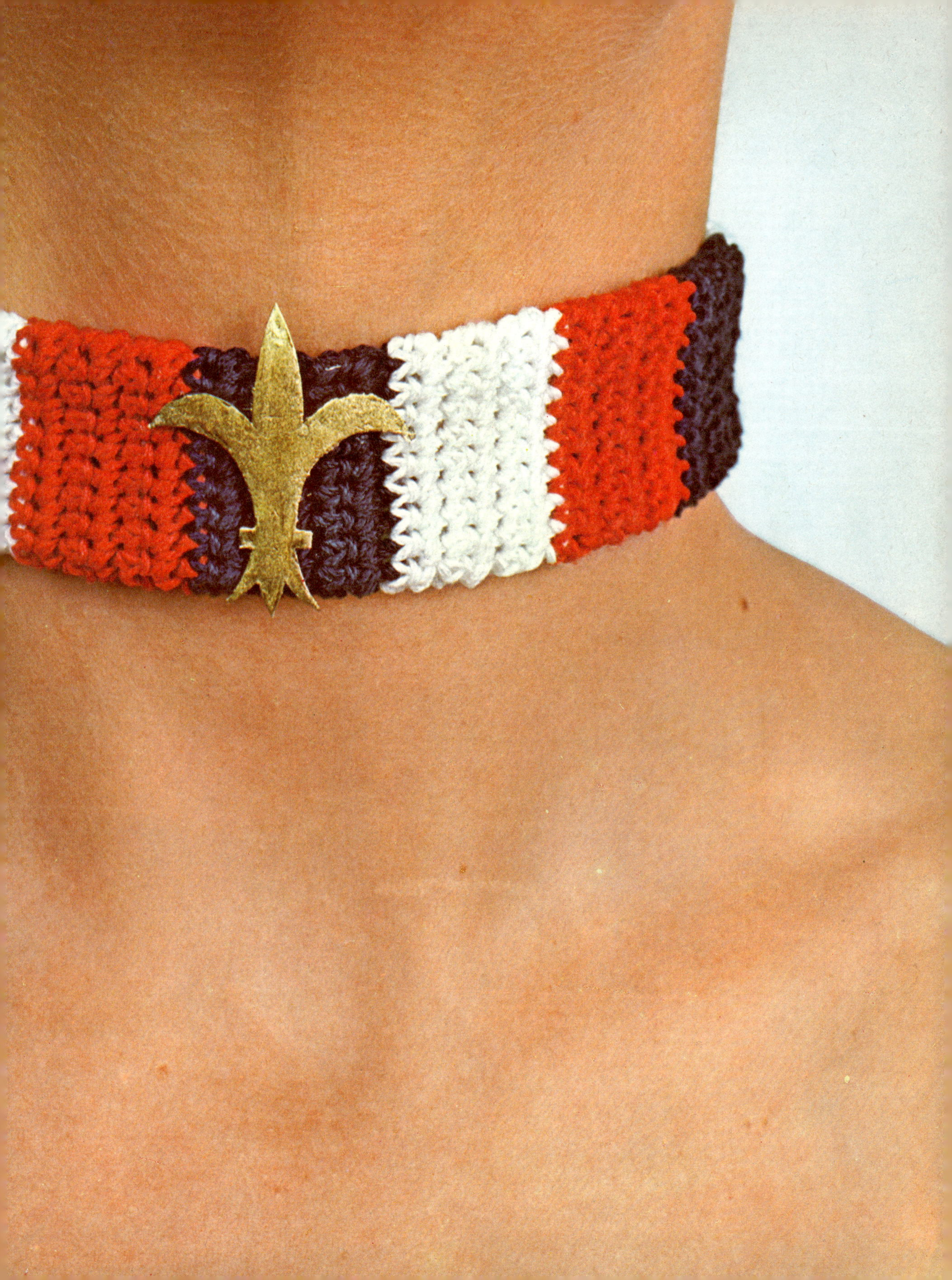

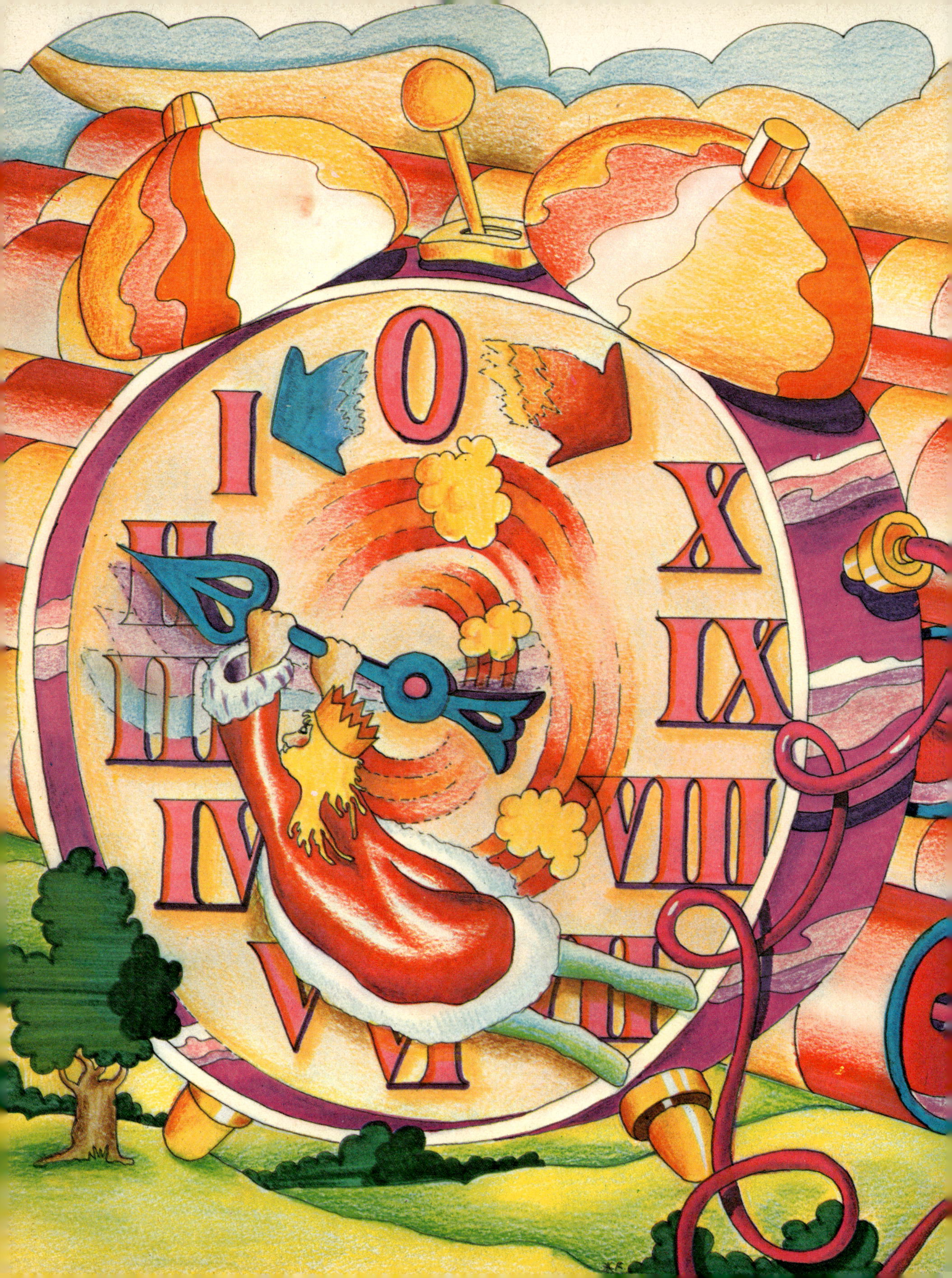

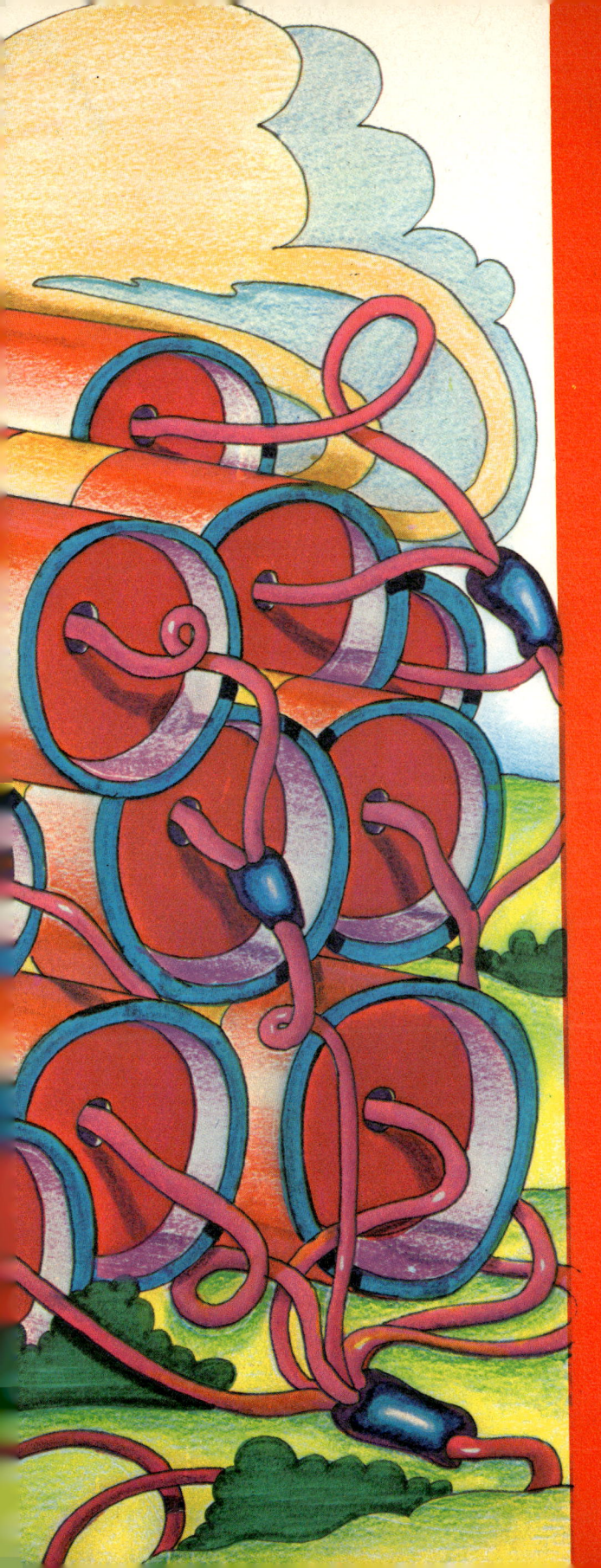

Sitting on a time bomb

The year 1848 was one of revolution all over Europe. All the worst fears of kings and politicians, and powerful middle class people came true. Governments collapsed, kings fled from their countries. From Paris in France to Budapest in Hungary, from Denmark in the north to Italy in the south, thousands of people roamed the streets shouting about freedom and independence. Only Russia and Britain escaped, although Britain came close to having its own revolution.

Ever since Napoleon had been banished to St Helena, the politicians of Europe had tried to stop the clock of progress. Under Prince Metternich, the old monarchs had been restored—that was a bit like putting the clock back!

But kings, governments, and everyone else who was against change and reform were sitting on a ticking time bomb. The countdown had begun. . .

There was no way to stop the clock. People everywhere were demanding their freedom, and they would not be satisfied until they gained it.

Red ivy

Ivy is a sturdy, hardy plant that has a very strong grip on life. It goes on sending out new leaves even when it is cut down, and it will grow again in the same spot even when it is pulled up by the roots. People are like the ivy plant. They will live through extremely hard times, fight in wars, survive revolutions, and give birth to new generations of people. Like the ivy plant, the human race can survive almost any hardship.

The ivy in the picture is coloured red for two reasons. Red is traditionally the colour of war and bloodshed. Red is also, traditionally, the colour of revolution. When people try to gain freedom and more liberty, they often resort to bloodshed.
Before the twentieth century few countries and few people gained their freedom without bloodshed. Kings, noblemen, and powerful statesmen resisted strongly when people began to demand more freedom. In Europe especially there have been many wars and riots and revolutions in which the people suffered terribly. With the end of Napoleon's career, a new age began—an age when people began to try to live and work together more peacefully. New forces of goodwill were needed for individual people and individual countries to progress towards a more civilized and humane society. New machines were being invented and new methods thought up of doing the old work. The Industrial Revolution, that would change the way of life of a great many people, was about to begin.

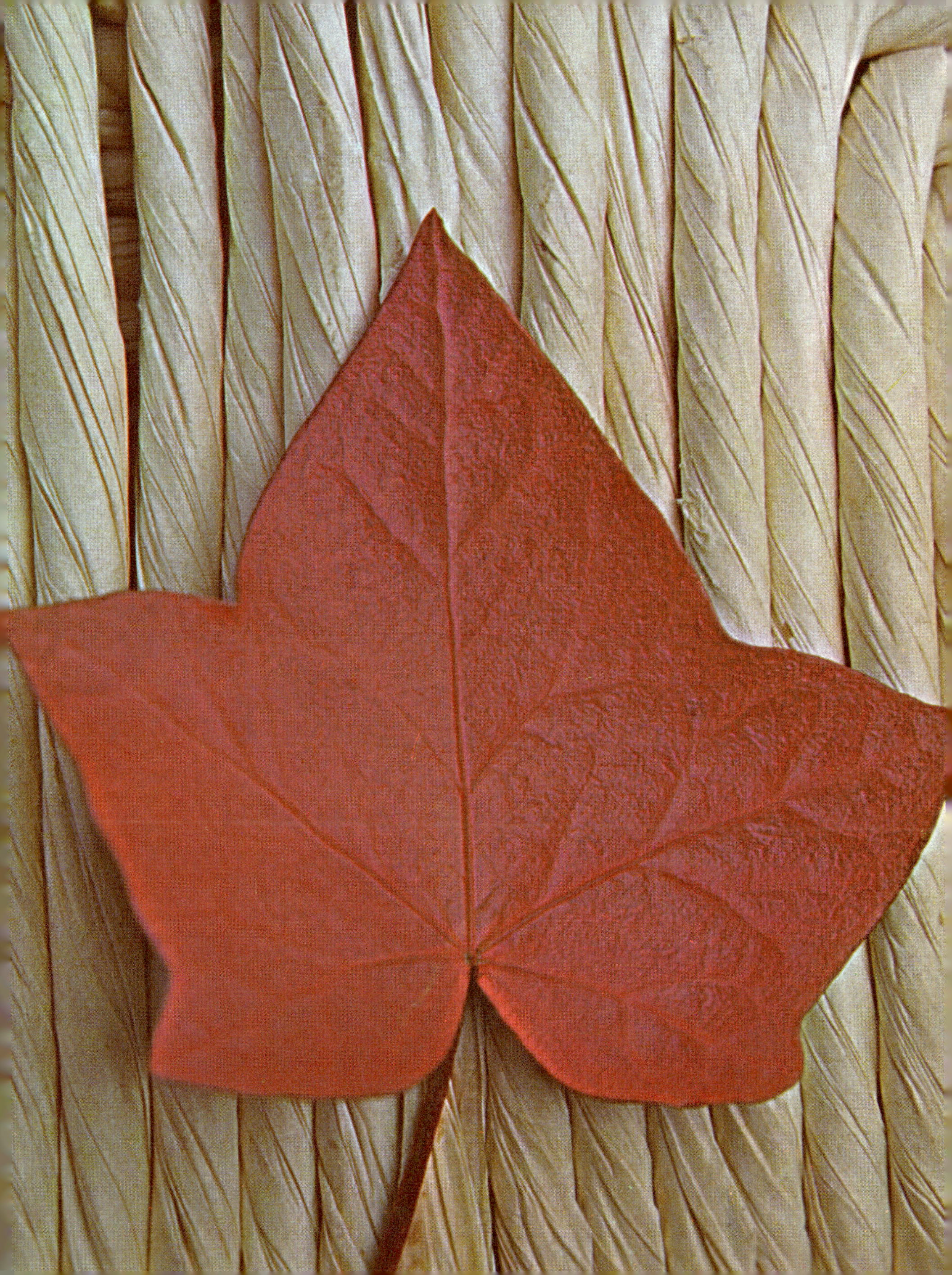

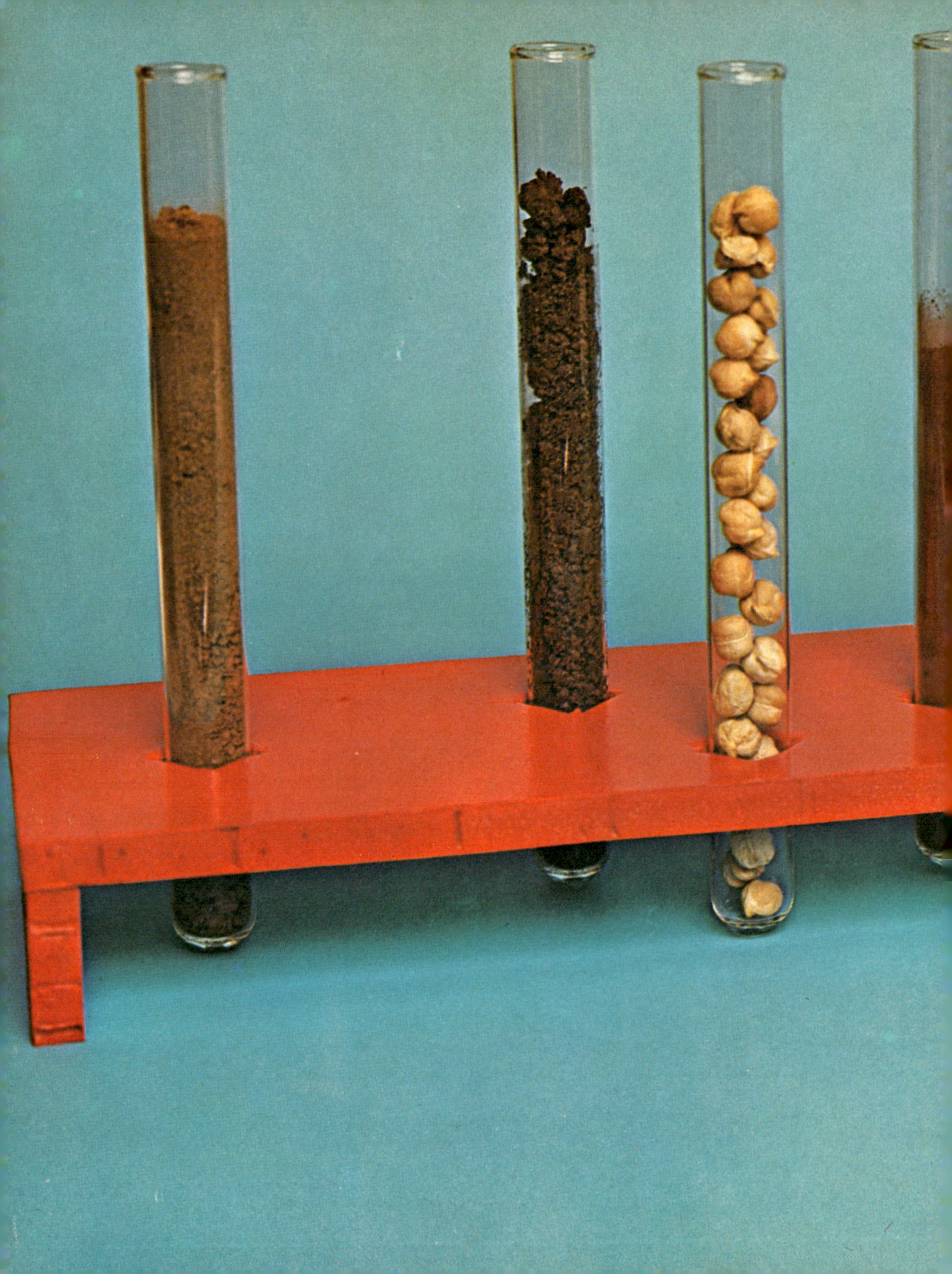

The agrarian revolution

An early factor that led up to the Industrial Revolution was the change in the ways of growing food. This was an agrarian or agricultural revolution. At the beginning of the nineteenth century, farmers sowed seeds by hand and cut crops with scythes. Today, they use machines on farms for sowing, cutting and reaping the crops. Farmers depend on scientists working in laboratories with test tubes to help them grow more food in more efficient ways.

Working life changes

The growing and harvesting of food crops is the most important type of work. Agriculture (working the land) is also one of the oldest forms of work. When the first hunters and fishermen settled in various parts of the world to grow crops, man had started on the path to civilization.

Up until the nineteenth century, most people who worked were farmers. Then inventions and discoveries made it possible for fewer people to grow more food. This freed farm workers to work in new jobs created by the invention of new machines. In a very short period of time (about one hundred and fifty years) a new kind of revolution changed the way of life and the ways of working of a great number of people in many parts of the world. This was the Industrial Revolution, a startling change in working life. This revolution, or profound change, transformed modern day life.

The country which led the world in the Industrial Revolution was Britain. The scarecrow in the picture is handsomely dressed in top hat and tails. He is obviously much better off than the usual raggedy scarecrow. The British farmer was like the handsome scarecrow. New methods of sowing seeds, gathering crops, and working the land made British farmers much better off than farmers in other countries.

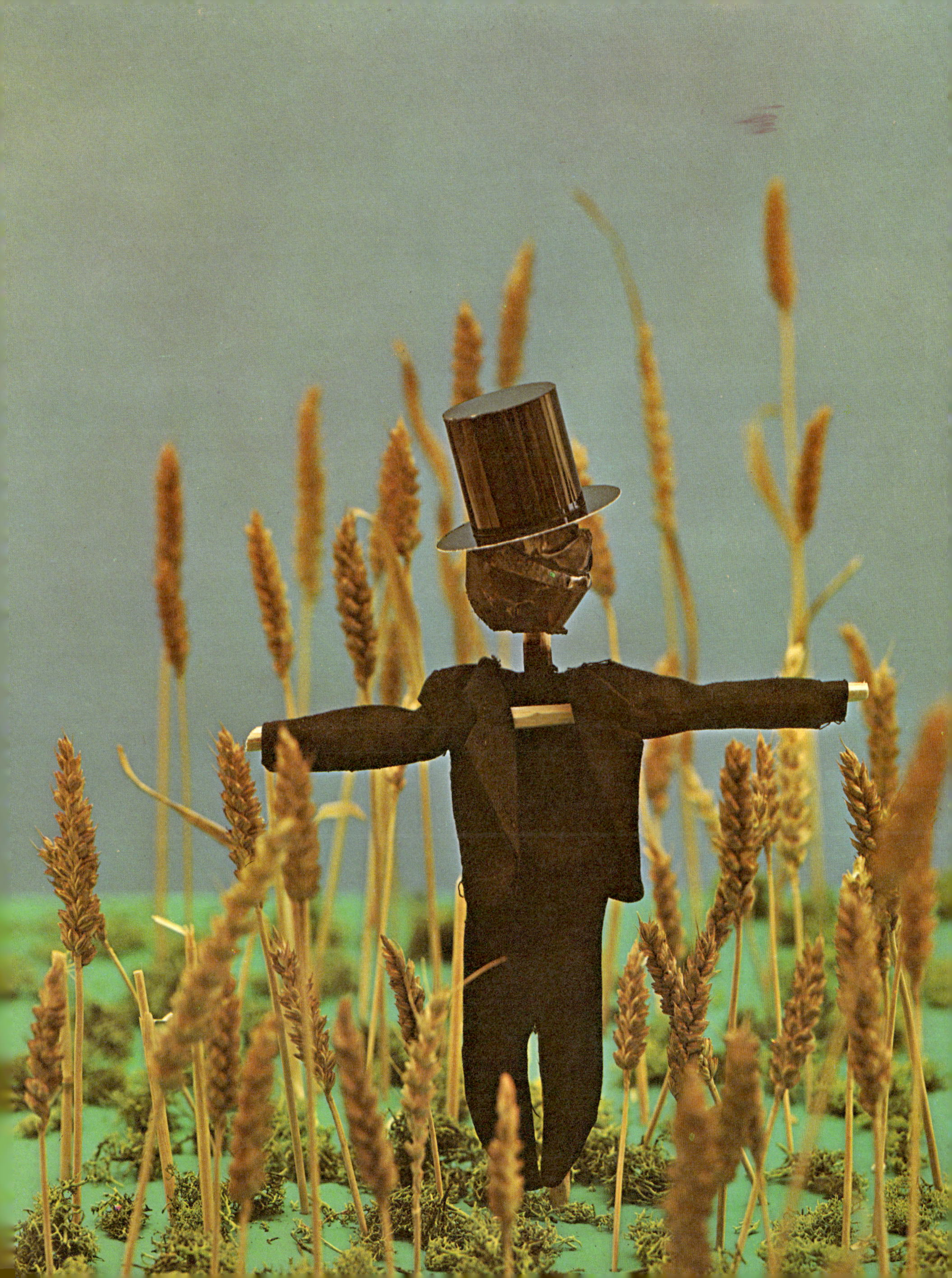

Water power

As the Industrial Revolution got under way, more and more new machines were invented to do all sorts of work.

At first factories and other places of work were set up near rivers because of the importance of water power. This was used to make the new machines work. This was the dawning of the age of steam—a development which pushed forward the many changes at an ever increasing pace.

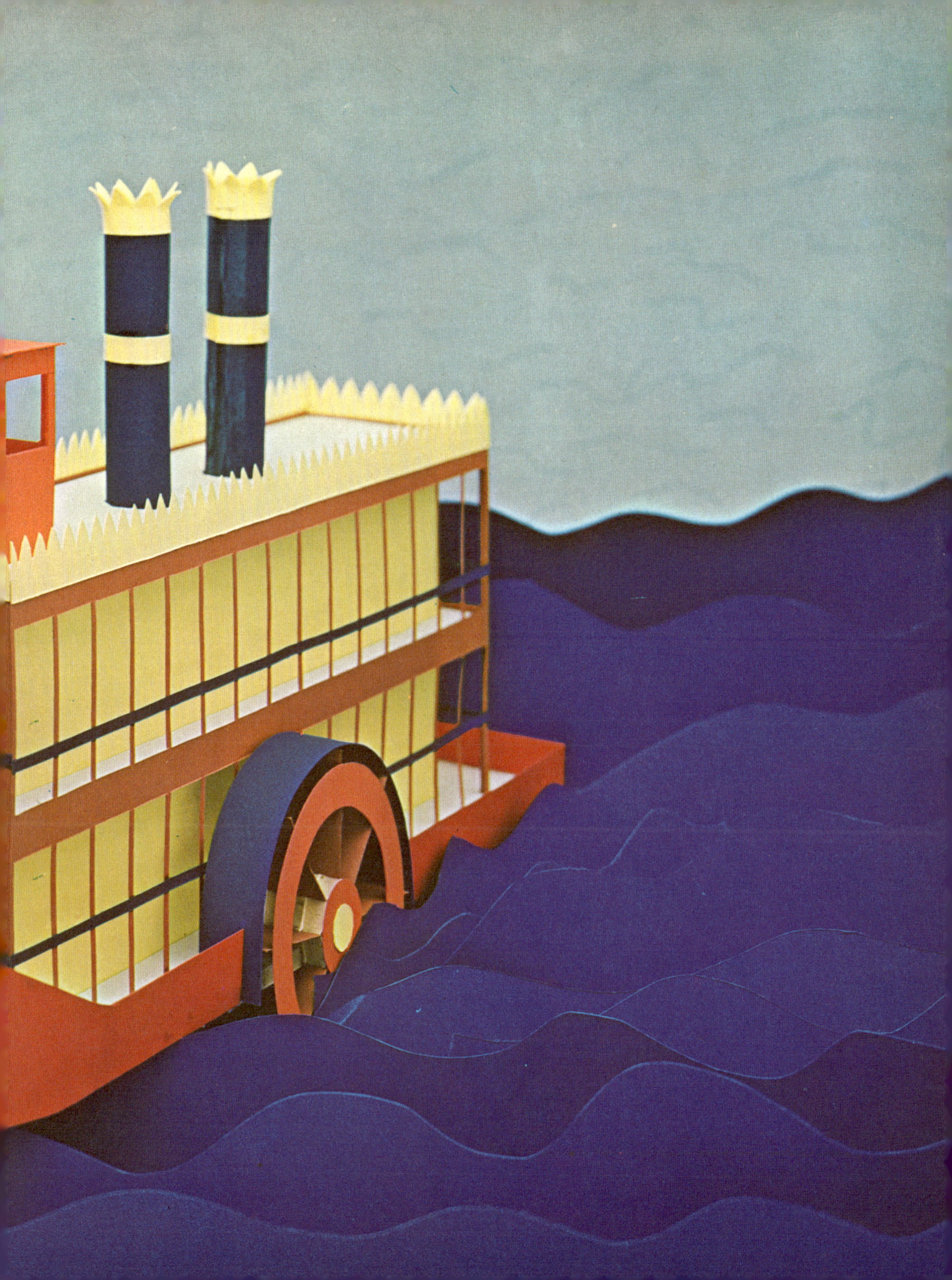

From water to coal

Among the first machines to be driven by water power were weaving looms and the "spinning jenny" for spinning thread. In England, steam engines were first developed to pump water out of coal mines. Then in 1769, a Scotsman called James Watt greatly improved them. Soon steam engines were being used in factories. Suddenly coal was needed in huge quantities to heat the water to make the steam to drive the engines. Steam power paved the way for a big increase in the production of goods in factories. Men, women and children left the land to work in factories and live in towns.

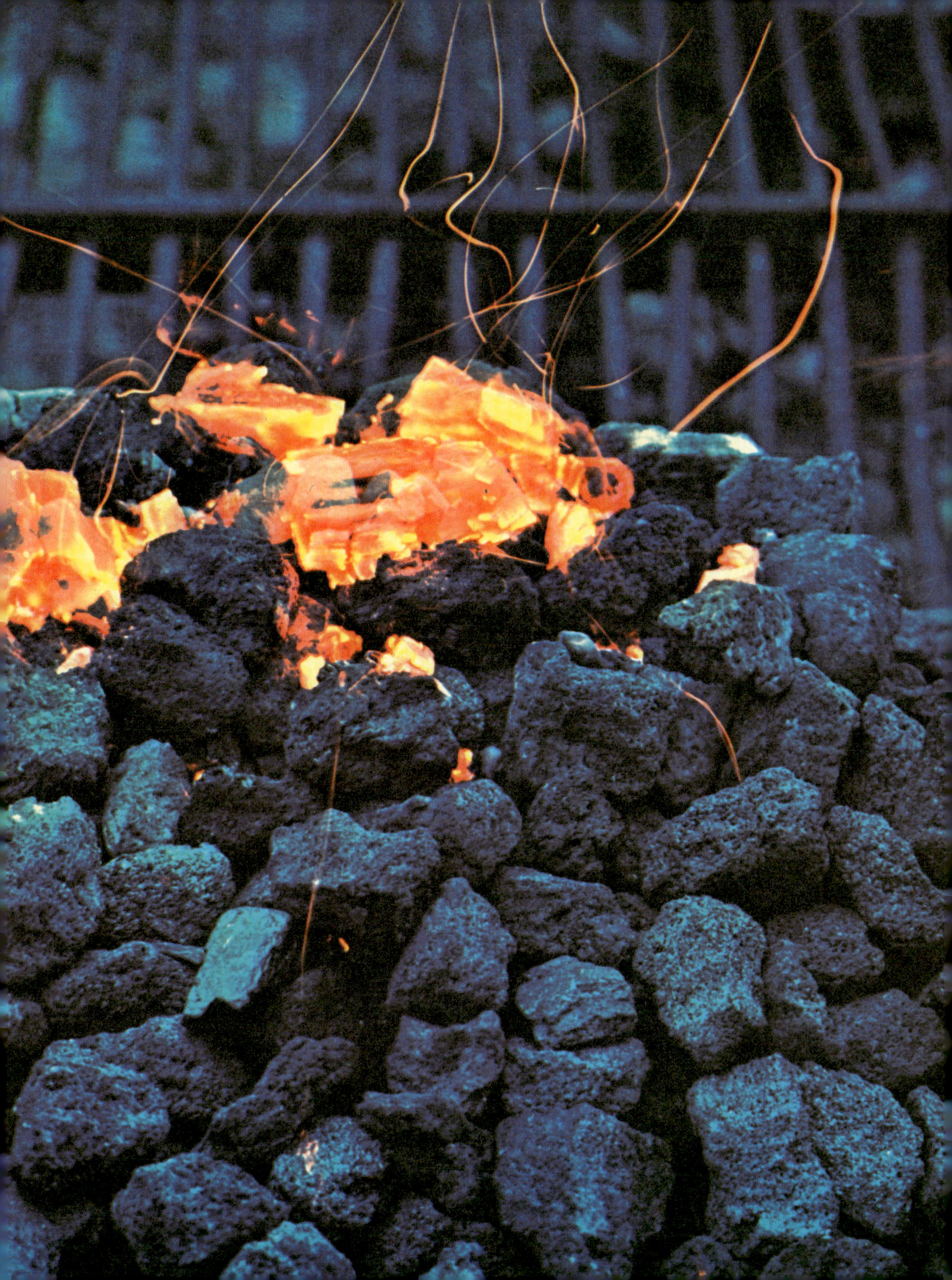

Swallowing up the people

By the late eighteenth century, man had made machines to work for him. Machines could do a lot of the jobs that people had had to do before by hand. But in a way men and women became the slaves of the machines. They flocked to the towns where the engines were providing new and different kinds of work.

Towns grew up round factories. People left the clean, healthy countryside where machines were doing a lot of the farm work they had done by hand. Cotton mills, iron works, coal mines and even the factories where the machines were made needed more and more workers. The gates opened wide and people flooded in looking for work. The factories swallowed people in huge numbers. And once they were inside it was very hard for them to escape. Wages were very small and whole families had to work almost non-stop to keep body and soul together. They worked long hours in terrible conditions to buy the small amounts of food and the few rags of clothing they could afford.

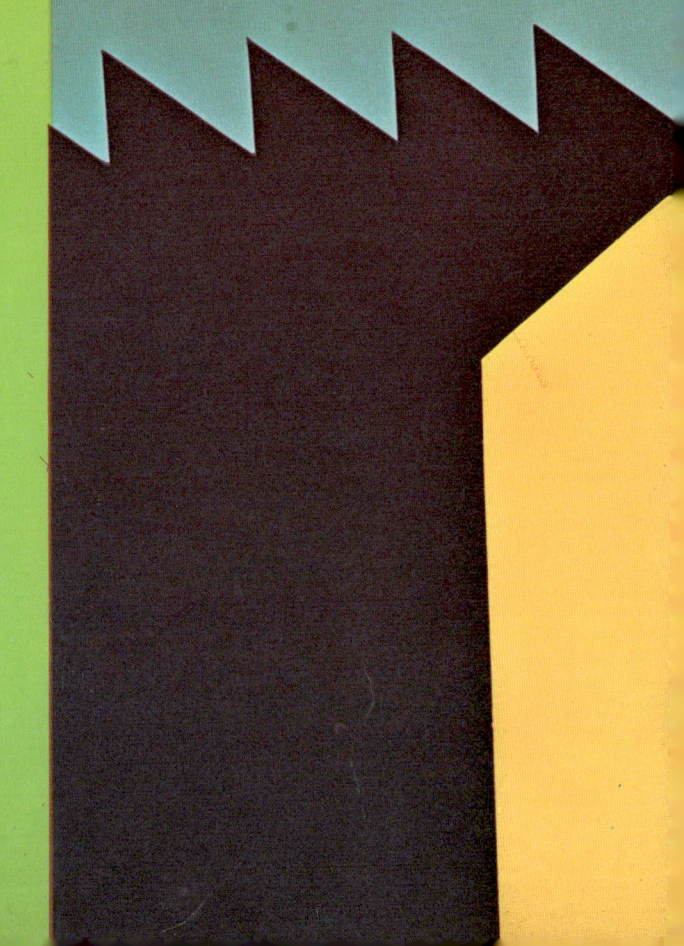

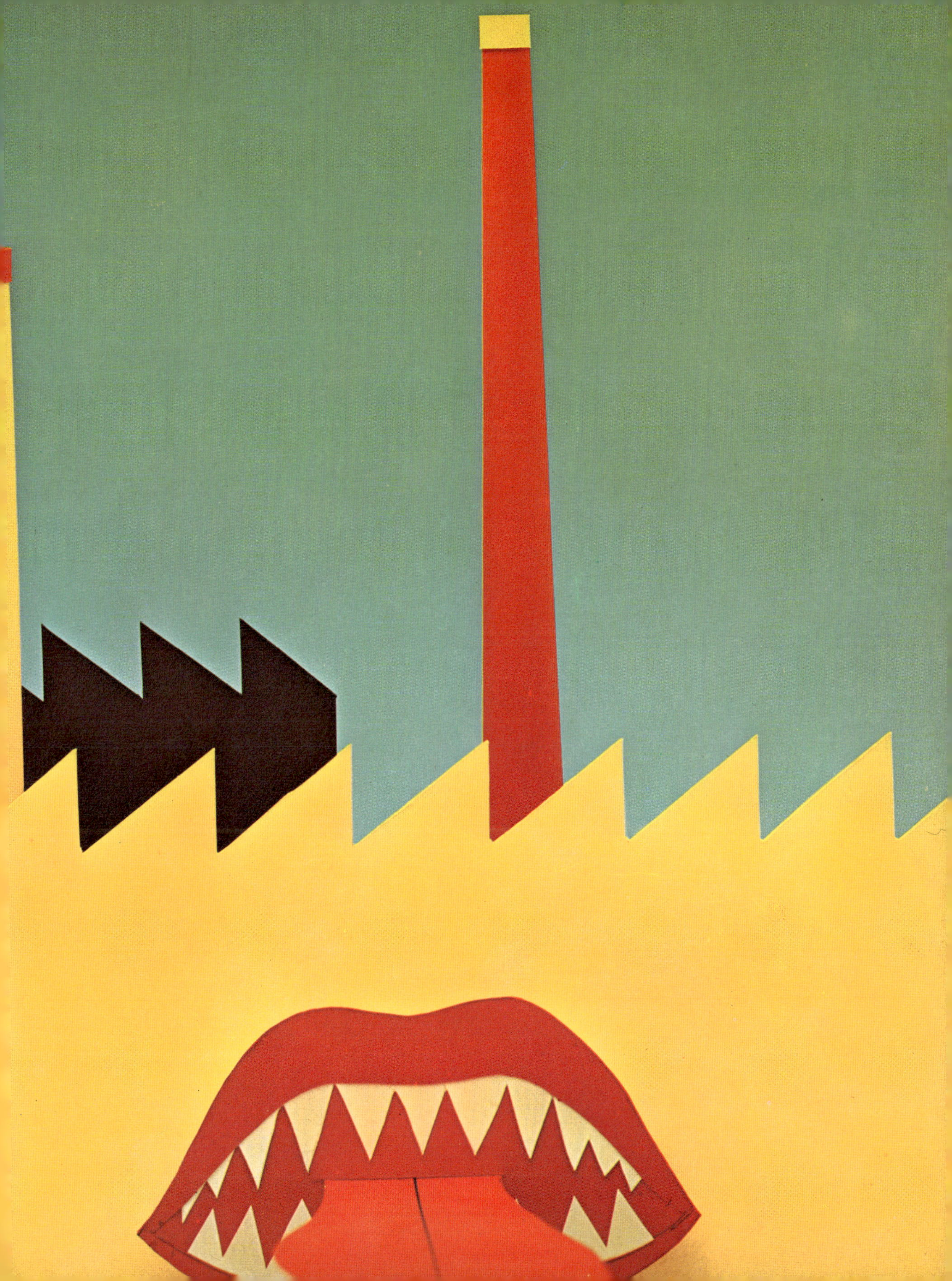

From legs to wheels

The Industrial Revolution was speeded up by new inventions in transport. In 1820 the first railway was constructed in England. People and goods could then travel longer distances faster than ever before. Four-legged animals were used less and less. The pace of life was speeding up—and legs were not as fast as wheels.

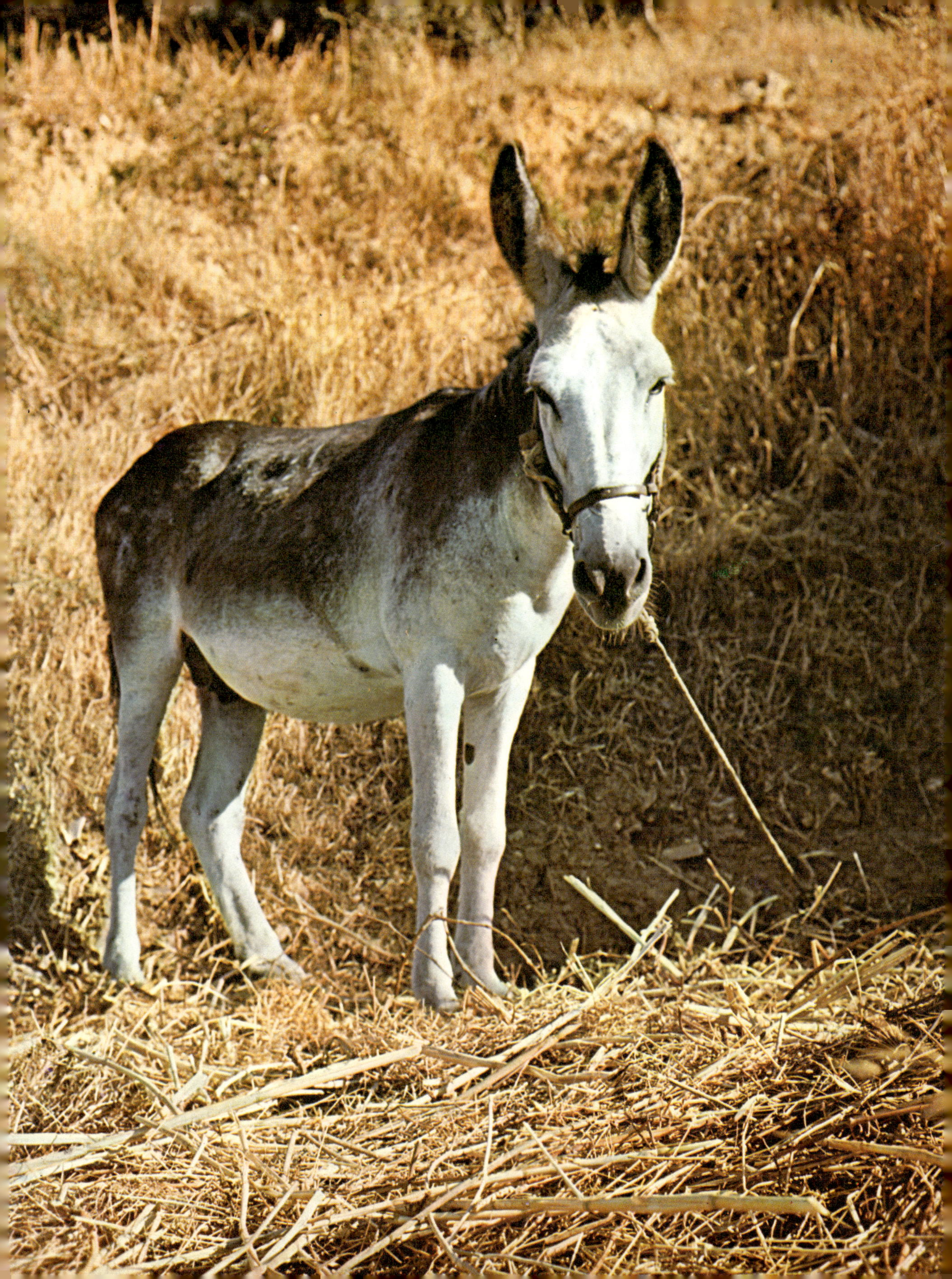

Tools make slums

Before the Industrial Revolution, most things were made by individual workmen working in their own cottages or in small workshops. Things changed when machines were invented to speed up the work. A machine is really a large, fast tool. Working alone a man might use a tool to turn a screw or tighten a bolt. A steam- or electrically-driven engine can tighten many bolts at the same time. New tools changed people's lives.

The nineteenth century saw the rapid growth of slums. As workers poured in from the country and were swallowed up in the factories, no attempt was made to give them a decent place to live. Overcrowding was one result of progress. Ugly, badly built houses were put up so close together that there was no space between houses. Smoke and soot belched out from the factories over the houses. The men who had been farmers and who had sought more money and an exciting new, free life with new kinds of work, found themselves living in filthy slum towns.

Telephone business

The telephone was one invention which helped factories and businesses to expand. Imagine the shields on the telephones are the symbol of a company. All over the world, telephones would link the company's offices. An employee of the company in Paris could talk to an employee of the company in London. Because business could be done by 'phone quickly, the company would make more money and so grow bigger.

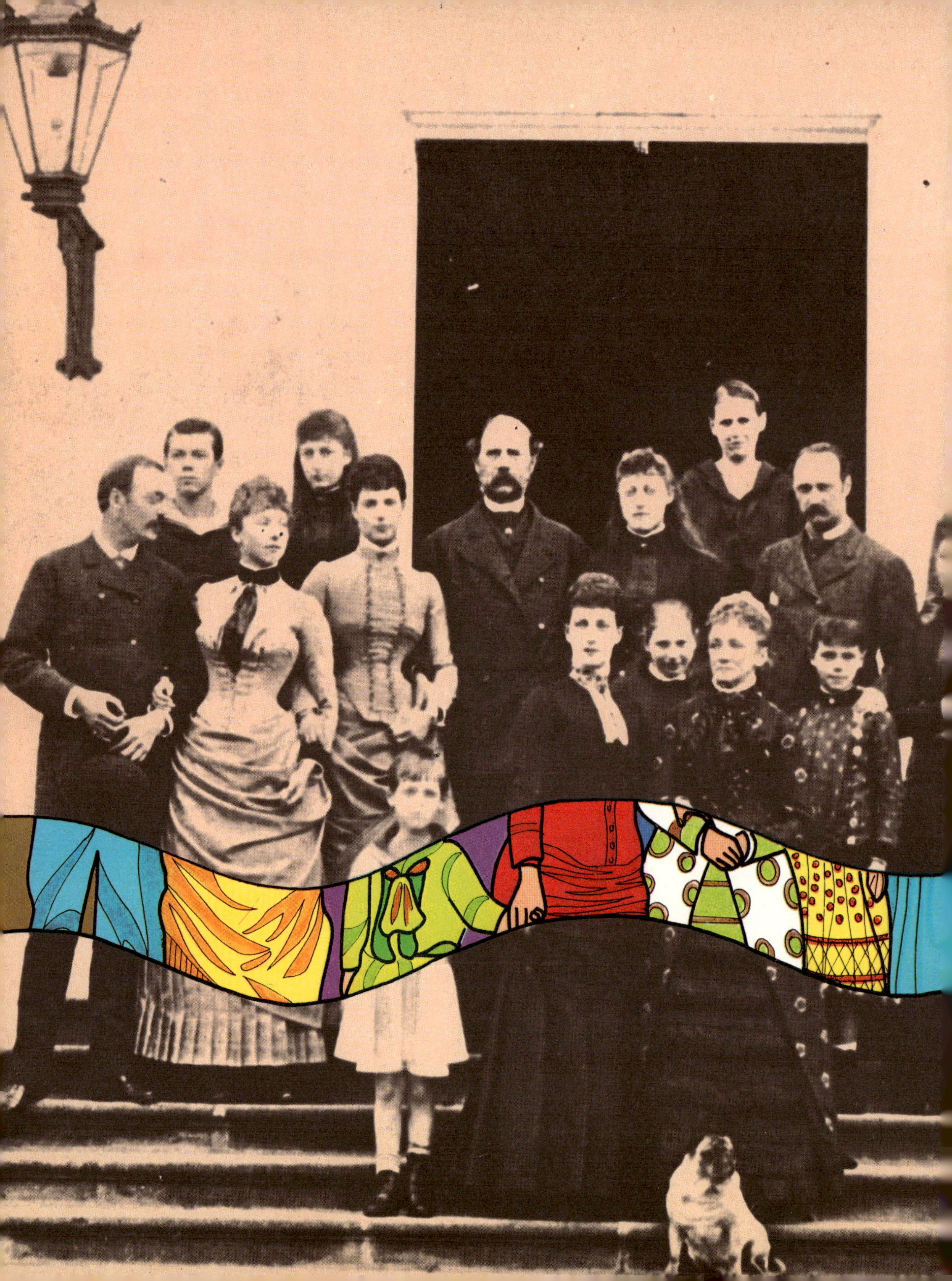

Men and Ideas

Long ago in the eighteenth and early nineteenth centuries, people were kept within the narrow bands of their class—for instance, a weaver did not move from his class into the landowner's class. But in the latter part of the nineteenth century, a new, colourful band appeared and grew ever wider. The man we call self-made had come upon the working scene—a man who could better his own life if he wished. He could be born a peasant and become a craftsman, businessman, or a banker.

People no longer believed that if a man and his family were born poor that there was no hope. Now people thought they could achieve a better life by their own hard work. Life could become richer, more colourful. Poor boys could become millionaires and powerful industrialists. New freedoms and new opportunities were there for all men to grasp.

As these self-made men grew ever more successful they took along with them other men, and so the colourful band of these early industrialists grew ever wider.

A new idol

As people began to see that they themselves could become richer, they began to attach more and more importance to money. Gold, the world's most precious metal, was the new idol for many. Getting more gold became a goal in life, for individuals and for nations. Gold bars became false gods, objects for worship, for pieces of paper currency were worth so much gold.

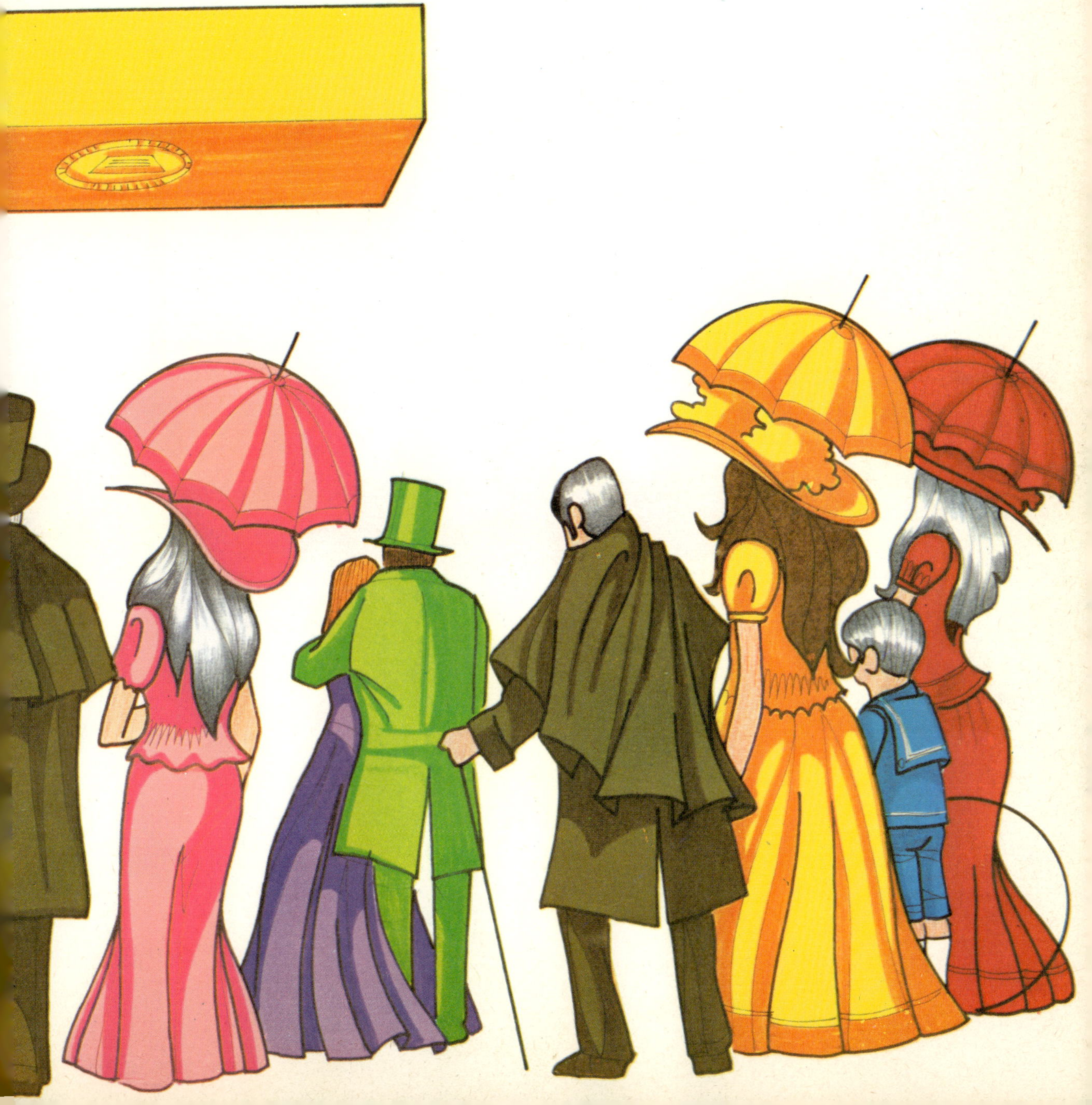

Light and dark

The beacon of the new freedom swept round the world in the nineteenth century. In some places the beacon shone with a bright light, in others dark patches remained. In North America there was great hope that every man would achieve his own freedom and be able to enjoy a happier, more decent way of life. In Europe, the new middle class people felt the new freedom most deeply. They believed above all that they should be free to make as much money as possible with no interference. The new businessmen and new industrialists believed that freedom meant they could run their businesses as they thought fit. This, of course, often kept working people from being free, especially if wages were low and working conditions were poor.

Freedom was now widely thought to mean material prosperity, which is a richness of manufactured goods. Economic, or money, freedom was very important to people. People saw freedom as the ability to buy better food, more expensive clothes, more furniture, and more goods of all kinds.

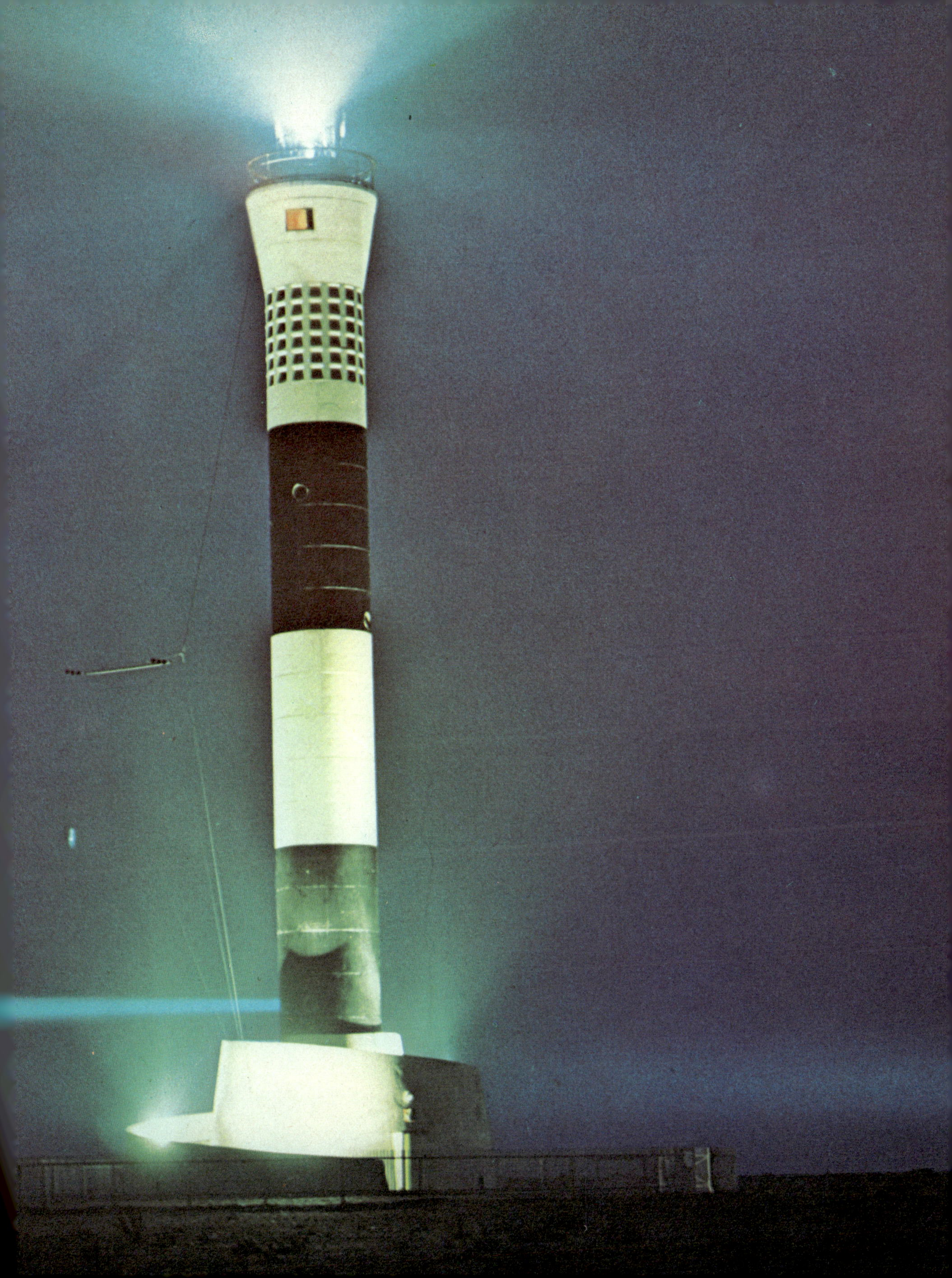

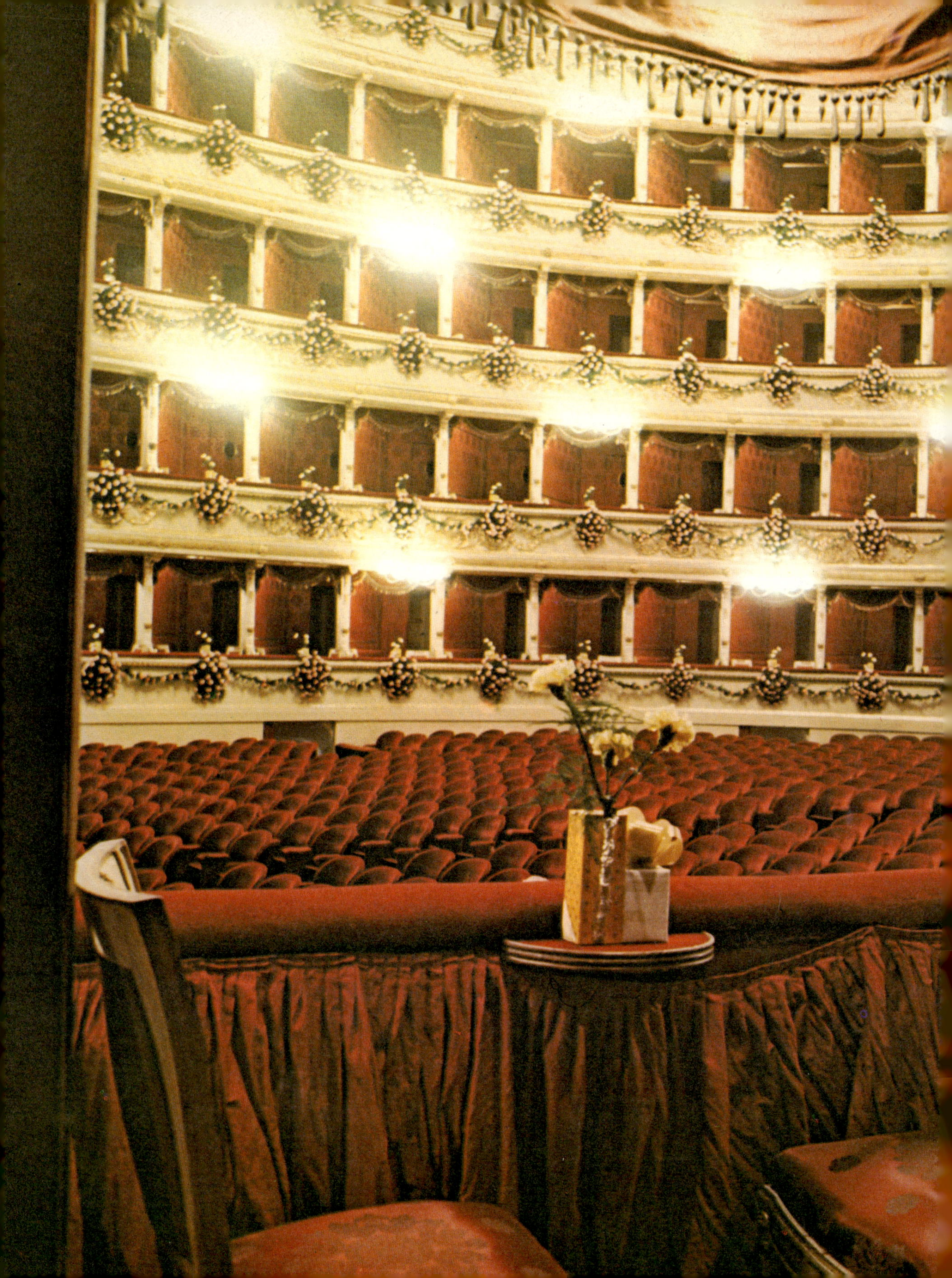

Power and pleasure

In this new industrial age, the big men of business, or industrialists, began to live a life much like the nobility of earlier centuries. With increasing wealth and increasing power, the new middle class people sought culture, education, and new leisure time activities. Money from newly rich men was spent on building luxurious theatres and opera houses. Poets, painters, writers, and sculptors found a new class of people willing and able to pay for their arts. In olden days, noblemen had paid for art and culture. In this new age, the middle class could afford to pay for culture. Schools and academies were built with middle class money. Scholars, teachers, and scientists found more and more people interested in learning from them. Exhibitions were very popular, and although they were often put on with the help of middle class money, all classes of society could go to see displays and shows of machinery, of works of art, of mechanical toys, and other products of the new age.

The brain and the pen

The picture shows a quill pen making a drawing of the electrical impulses given out by the brain. This picture of the brain's energy is called an encephalograph.

   Great thinkers and writers of the new age began to try to describe man and his emotions and activities in accurate detail. They could not yet record the electrical currents passing through the brain, as we can today. But they could study themselves closely and try to explain why people behave the way they do. New ideas in science and medicine helped the exploration of the human mind. The problems of society were now written about in a much more realistic way—all classes were written about, not just the noble and the rich. Plays, novels, poetry, as well as newspapers and magazines described the lives of ordinary working people. And the new middle class were the biggest market of all for this kind of material.

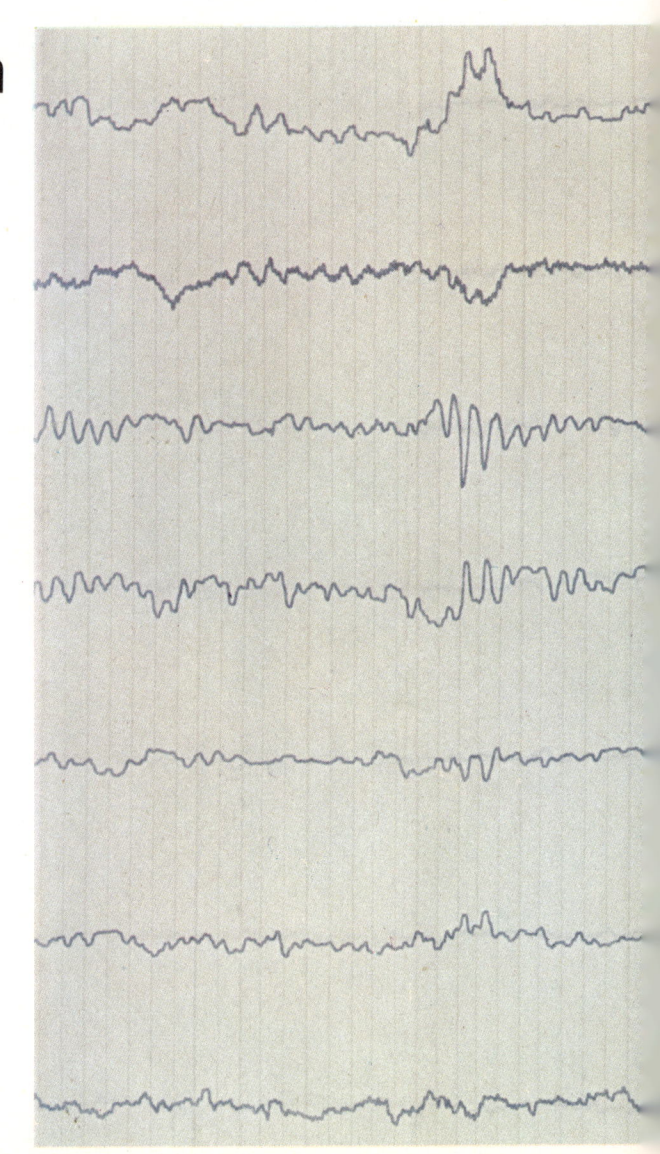

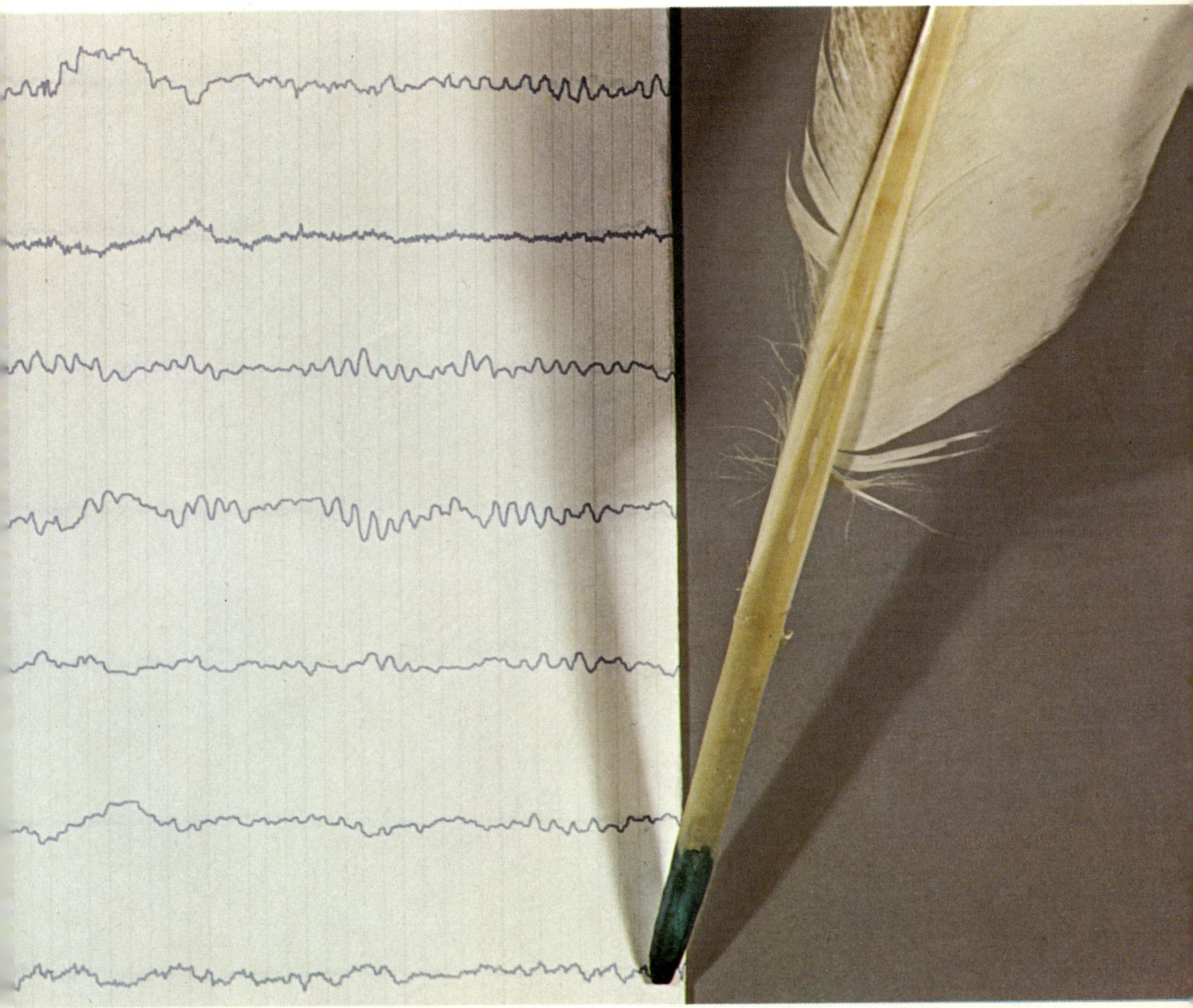

People in books

Writers began to describe the real life of everyday people in more accurate detail. As this happened, the newly rich middle classes began to see that perhaps all of life was not so free.

They began to understand that making money as freely as possible led to terrible hardships for many working people. The realistic novel led to a sympathy for those who were not so free or so fortunate, and slowly conditions were made better for working people.

The hooded falcon

Reforms or changes for the better came very slowly to the lives of everyday working people. The people who were fortunate enough to take advantage of the new age of machinery, and who made fortunes, often forgot how awful living conditions were for working people.

As new ideas travelled from country to country, more and more working people began to think and to wonder why they should live such hard lives. They saw the riches of the new middle class, and they began to be very unhappy. The masses of people began to see that it was possible to have a better way of life. They no longer had to wait and hope to go to heaven to reap rewards for their hard labour. By the year 1848 many people in Europe were in revolt. The old nobility and the new middle class were frightened, and from then on new laws began to be passed to make life for the common people healthier and better. The change was slow, however, for the masses of people were like a hooded falcon. If they did not see clearly that life could be decent, then they were not dangerous. Once a hood had been lifted from their eyes, then they would fight and kill their prey. And their prey was people better off than they who stood in the way of better living conditions.

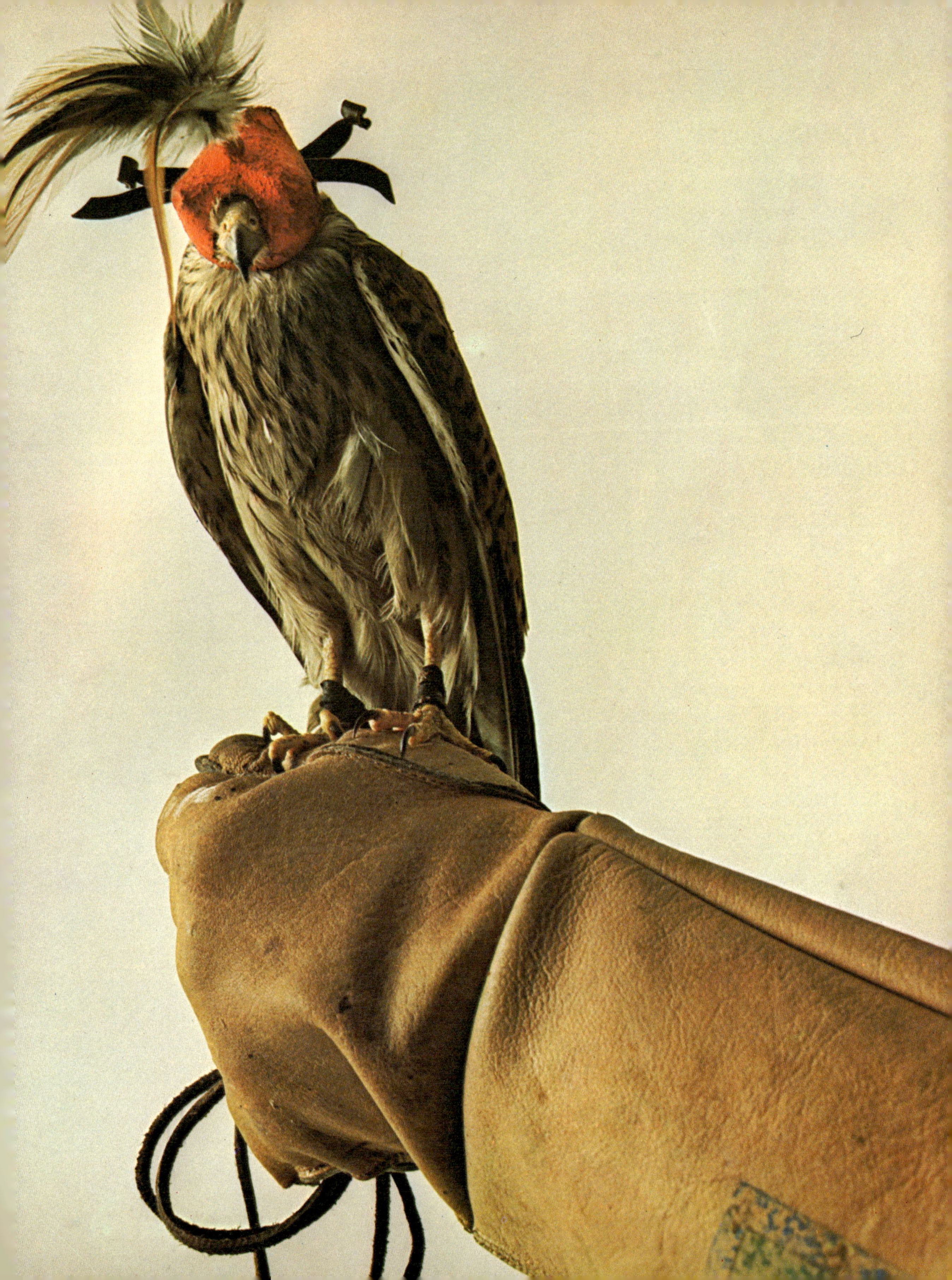

A new kind of European

As people found their way of life changing in the Industrial Revolution, they also began to have a different outlook on life. They had strong feelings of nationalism, or special pride in their own country.

In 1848 France faced another revolution. The working population were in a sorry plight and they took to rioting in the streets, hoping to overthrow the government. For a few days, they fought fiercely, but they were defeated by troops loyal to the king, Louis Philippe. Rather than face up to forming a new government, the old king abdicated or gave up his throne to his grandson, Louis Bonaparte. Louis made himself known to the French people. And after a new government was formed, modelled on the American government, a new president or head of government was to be elected by vote. Louis Bonaparte was elected by a huge majority of votes. People marked their ballots with a cross against his symbol—"N" because he was the Emperor Napoleon's nephew. The French people thought of their newly elected president as a democratic emperor.

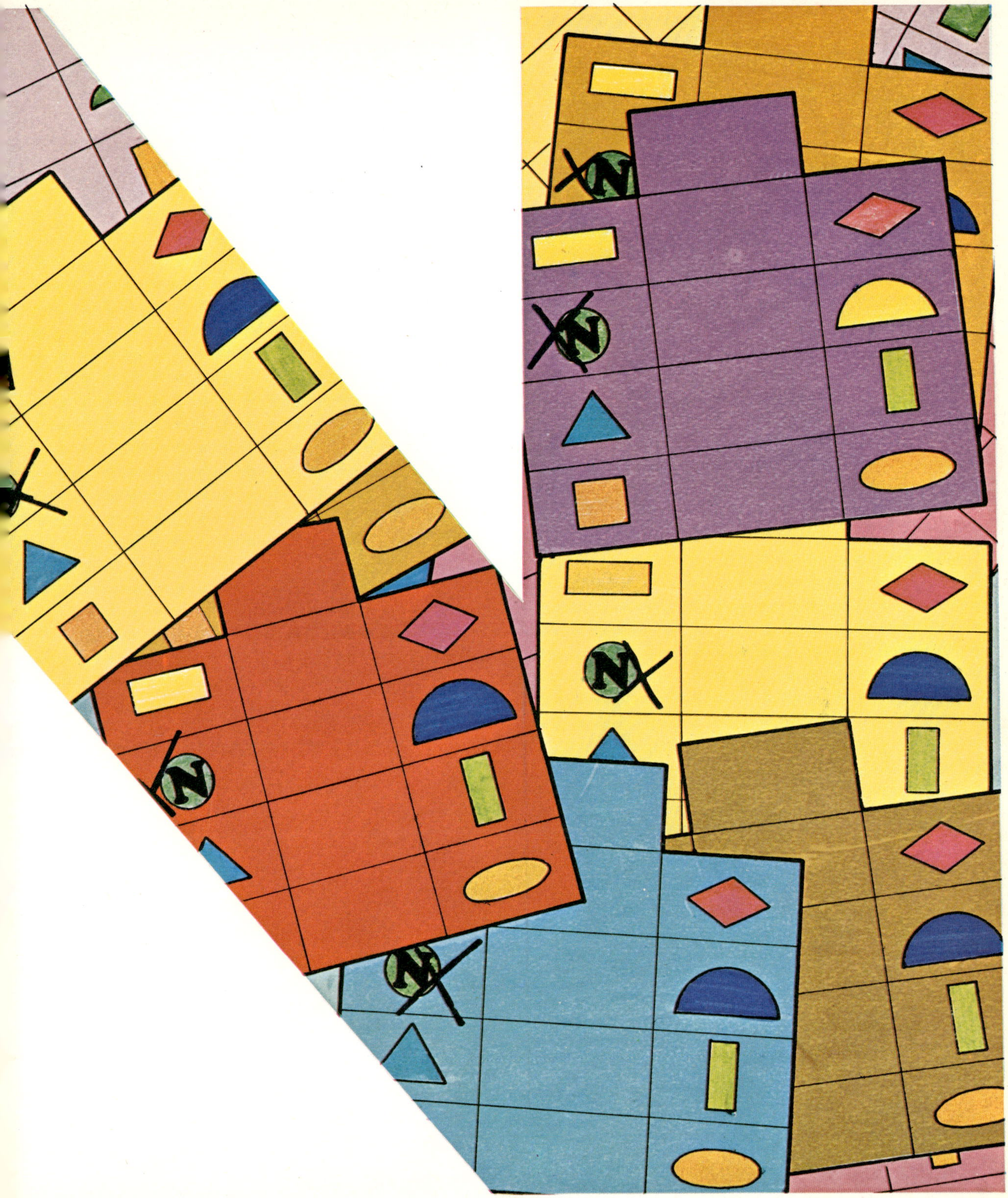

The people's friend in royal robes

When Louis-Napoleon Bonaparte became president of France, he was the people's choice and very popular. By 1848 when he was elected, the French had begun to dream of their past glories. The people were willing to riot and fight for their individual liberties, but they always looked back fondly at the former days when monarchs had put on a wonderful show of riches and pomp and when France had been a powerful empire. The name of Napoleon Bonaparte stirred people's imaginations. Now their new president was a Bonaparte too. Surely France would be glorious once again.

Louis-Napoleon pretended to be the people's friend, but he was ambitious for power and for glory. He had to rely on bankers and businessmen for money and support. Still he presented himself to the people as a man they could trust against the rich middle class. In his heart Napoleon knew he could keep the admiration of the French by following the same path as his uncle—the road to military glory and an empire. In 1851, Louis-Napoleon's great chance arrived. By trickery he restored the French Empire, called the Second Empire, and declared himself to be the Emperor of France, Napoleon III. The people's friend had stopped pretending and had become a royal monarch in the old style.

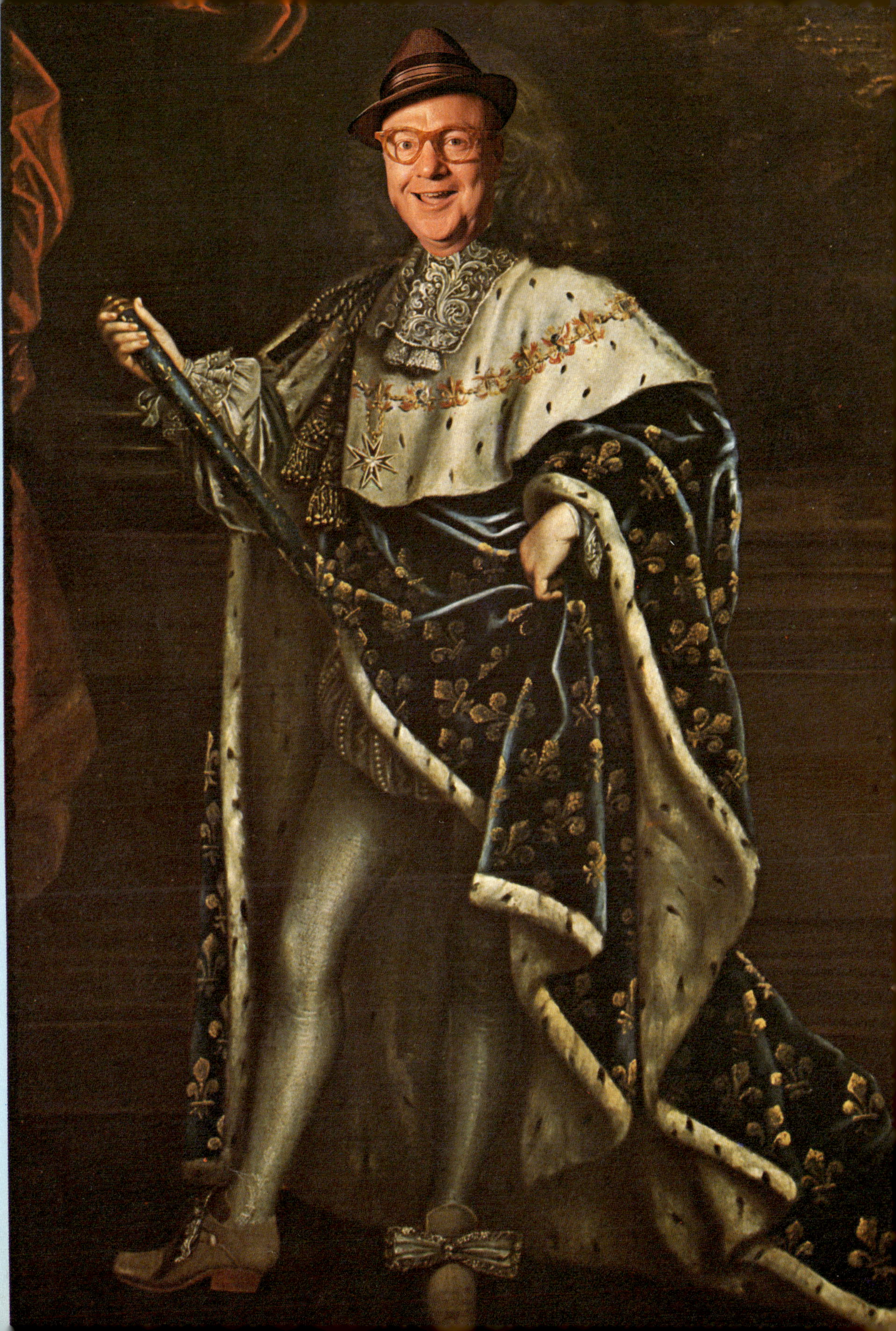

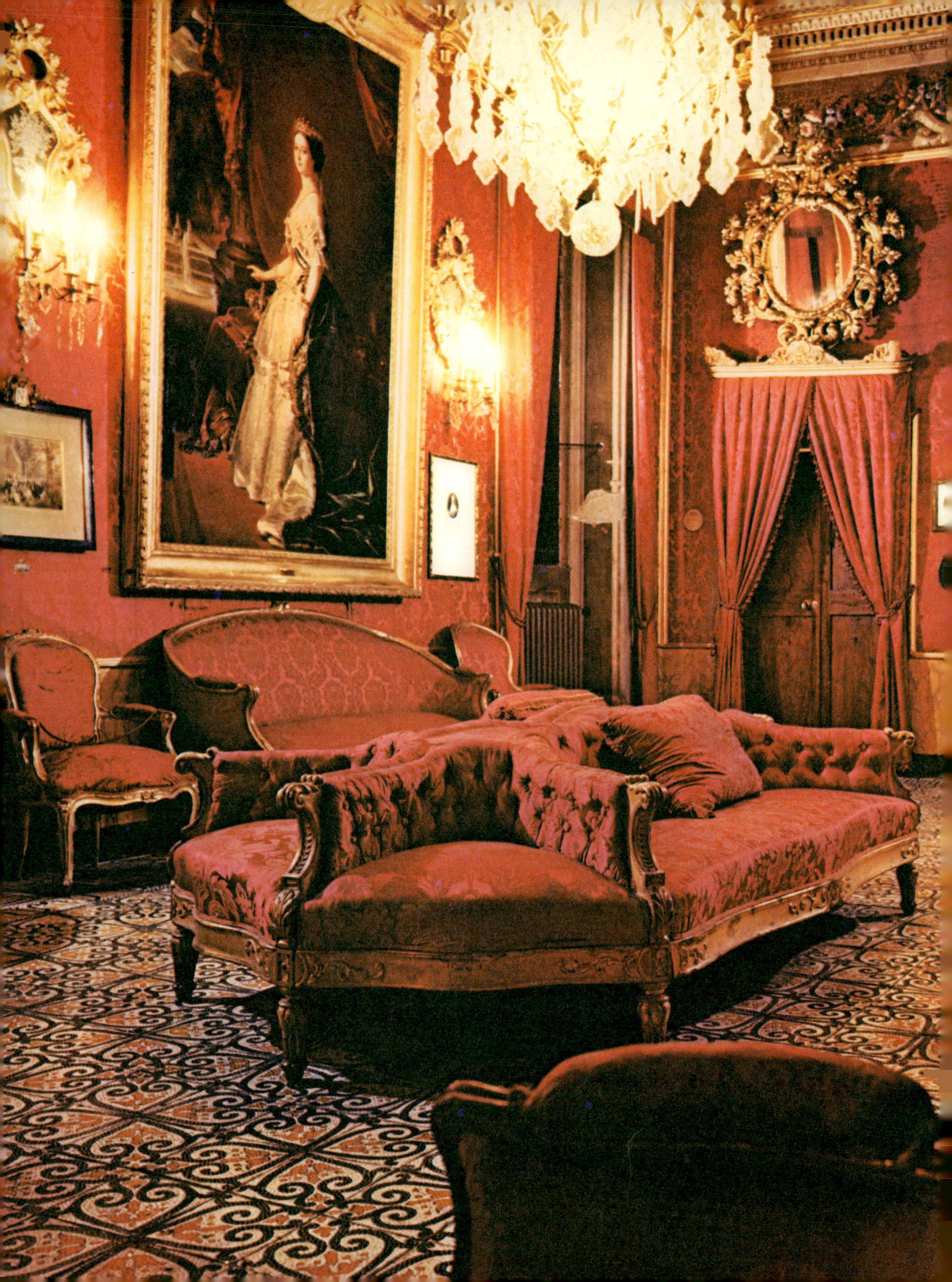

The Second Empire

Louis-Napoleon wanted to return to the glories of the French Empire. Under his rule, as Napoleon III, France gloried in the Second Empire. There was a royal court. Clothing and interior room decorations became elaborate. Paris was again a capital city of fashion. Napoleon III tried to expand French control over other parts of the world as his famous uncle had done. He was not very successful in his attempts to expand French power abroad. The French engaged in costly wars in Mexico and in the Crimea, the large island-like peninsula which juts into the Black Sea. There France and Britain fought with the Sultan of Turkey against Russia. France helped Italian armies in a war against Austria which resulted in a new Italian kingdom, but cost the French dearly.

One of Napoleon III's big successes was a great exhibition in 1867. Fifteen million visitors from all over the world travelled to Paris to view the exhibits. Included was a new metal, aluminium, which would have an important effect on the world since it was lighter than steel, and industrial products would become lighter and easier to use when made from the metal.

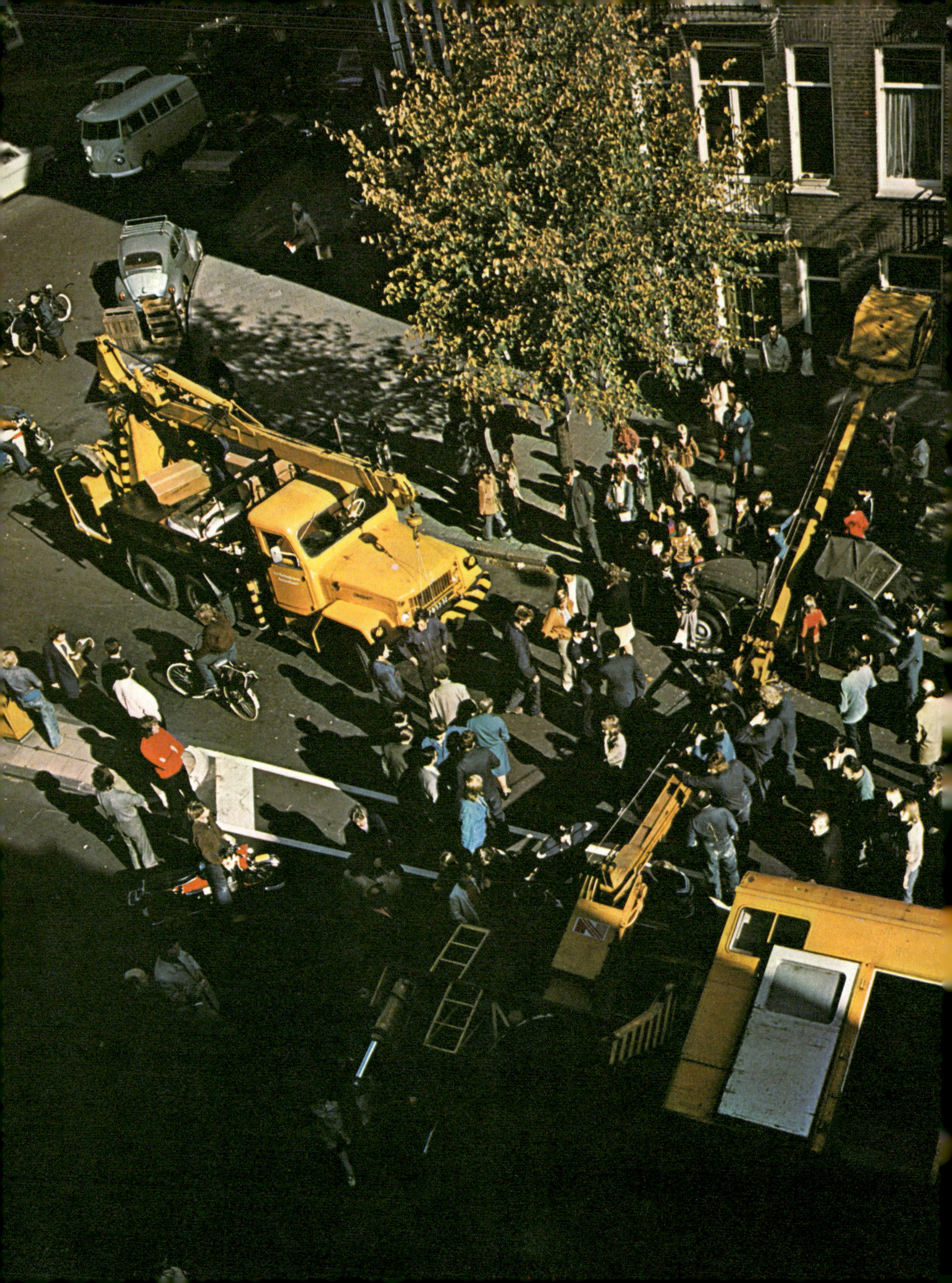

Man of accidents

Peace had reigned in Europe for some time. However, men became more interested in whether their own country was more powerful than other countries. In 1849 a German parliament met and decided the Prussian king should become emperor of all Germany. Then Austria set up a parliament of the old assembly of German states. Otto von Bismarck of Prussia attended, and he felt Germany should be strong and unified. Bismarck was a shrewd statesman. He began creating accidents and misunderstandings among European states to unite Germany. Bismarck gained the approval of the Prussian king.

The first "accident" was the invasion of two small Danish–German states, Schleswig and Holstein. They were brought under German control. Then Bismarck picked a quarrel with Austria over the two small states. In six weeks Prussia defeated all the Austrian armies and became master of northern Germany. All of Europe was surprised and shocked at the unexpected accident of war. There was little to do except stand and watch as Bismarck and Prussia cleared up the wreckage and took control of the situation, which was, of course, exactly what they had intended.

The new package

Within a few years, Bismarck was able to take all the separate German states and put them together to form a united Germany.

Northern and southern Germany, Austria and its surrounding lands bowed to Prussian military might. These territories were as different as glasses, plates, and bowls, but Bismarck tied the package together to make a strong new power in Europe.

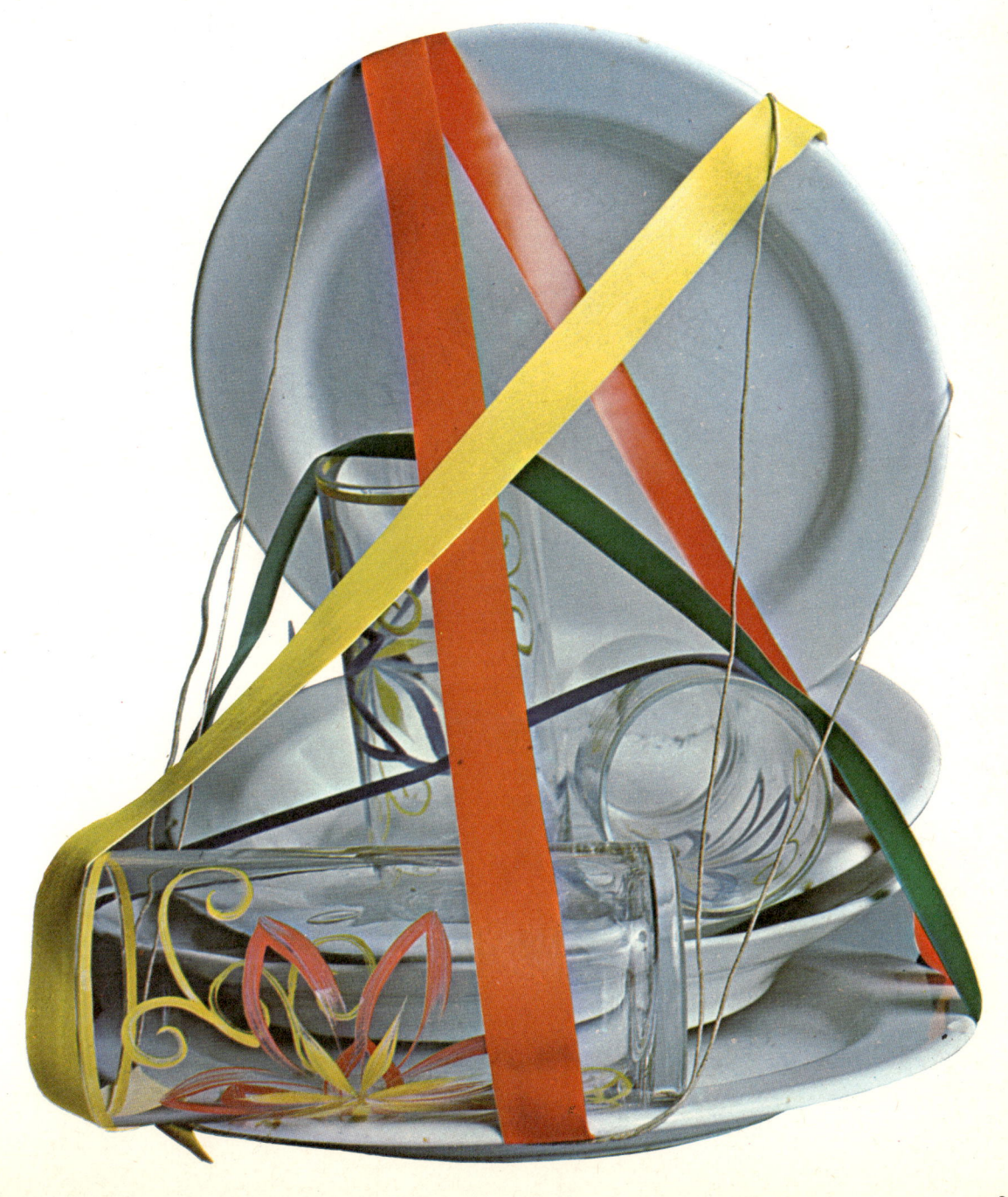

The hand on the controls

People did not realize exactly how or why the Germans had raced so quickly into becoming a nation. Bismarck was controlling them. He had old fashioned ideas. He believed in controlling the movements of men and governments from a distance. The boy in the picture in the old fashioned costume moves the modern racing cars by remote control. Bismarck ruled the German states by remote but powerful control.

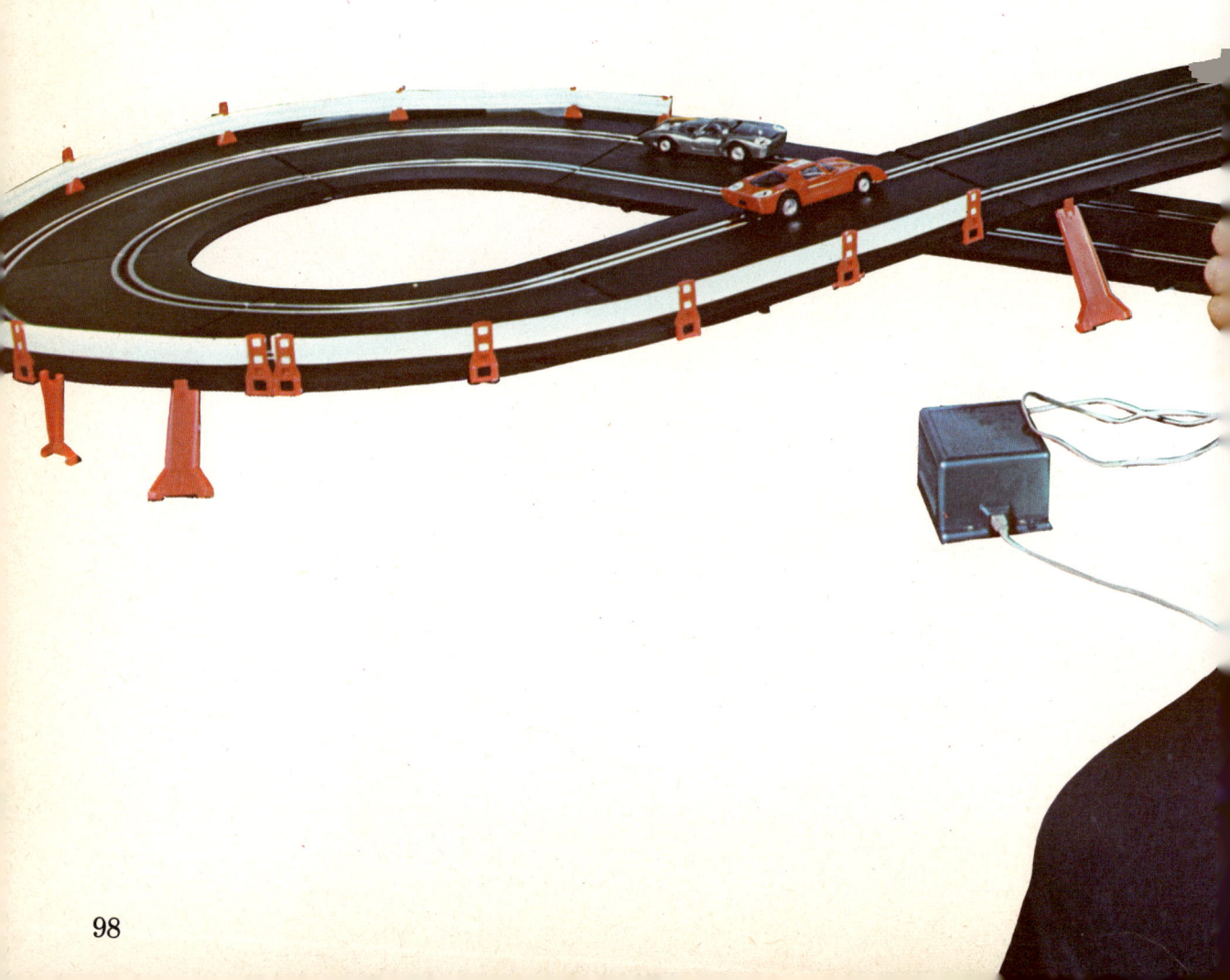

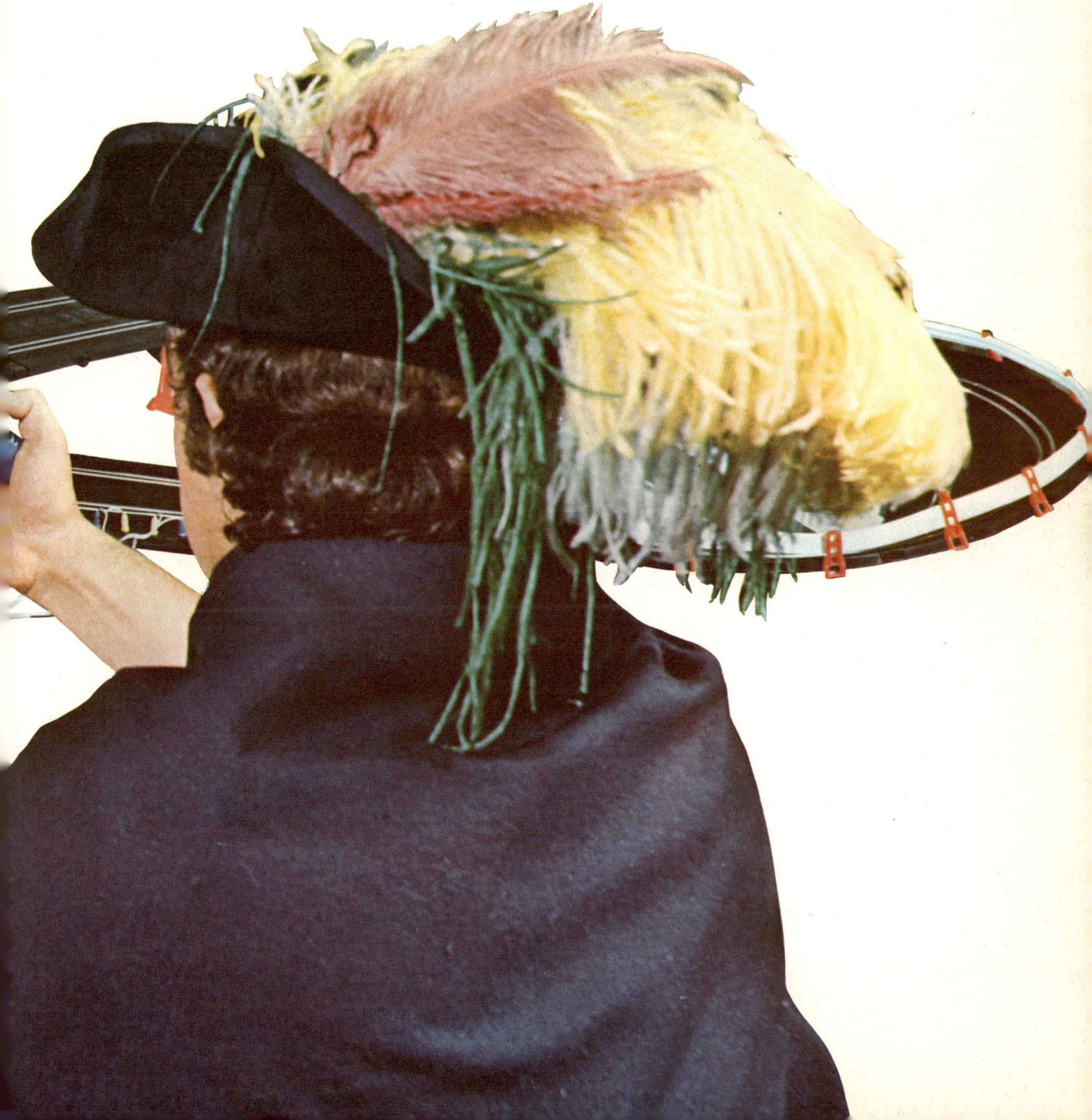

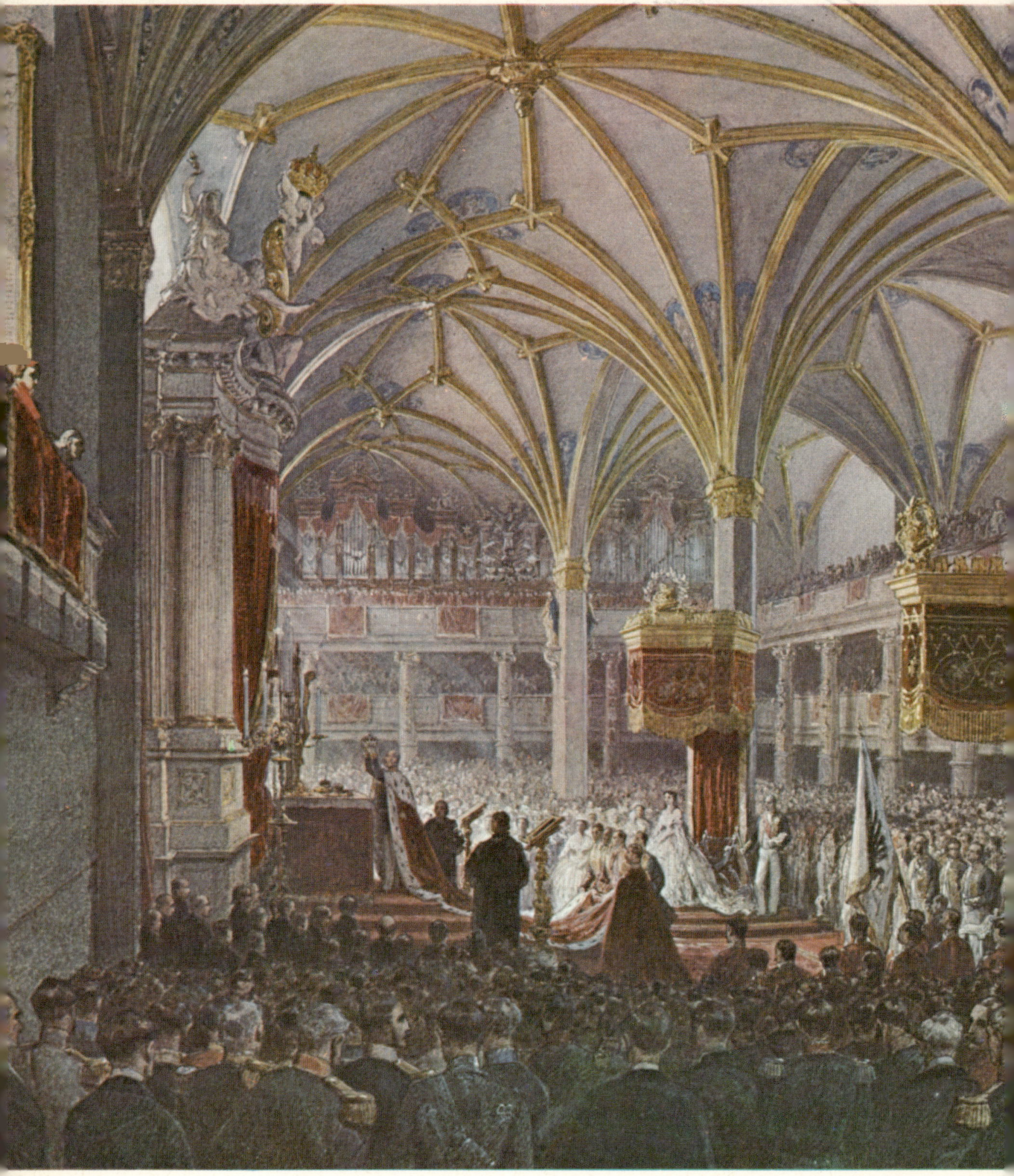

The final blow

The French and the Germans became serious rivals for power. Napoleon III thought a war with Germany would increase his power and popularity.

Bismarck obviously felt a war with France would help his plans for Germany. In 1870 they went to war over which ruler should sit on the Spanish throne. Germany won, and ten days before Paris fell, the king of Prussia was crowned Emperor of all Germany. The coronation was like a sledge hammer blow to France and to Europe. Now they realized a new German Empire had arisen.

A Nation Grows

The British colonists in North America had rebelled against the mother country in 1775. By 1781 they were free and independent. A new nation in a strange new world had come into being—the United States of America. The states grew rapidly into a power Europe had to reckon with.

103

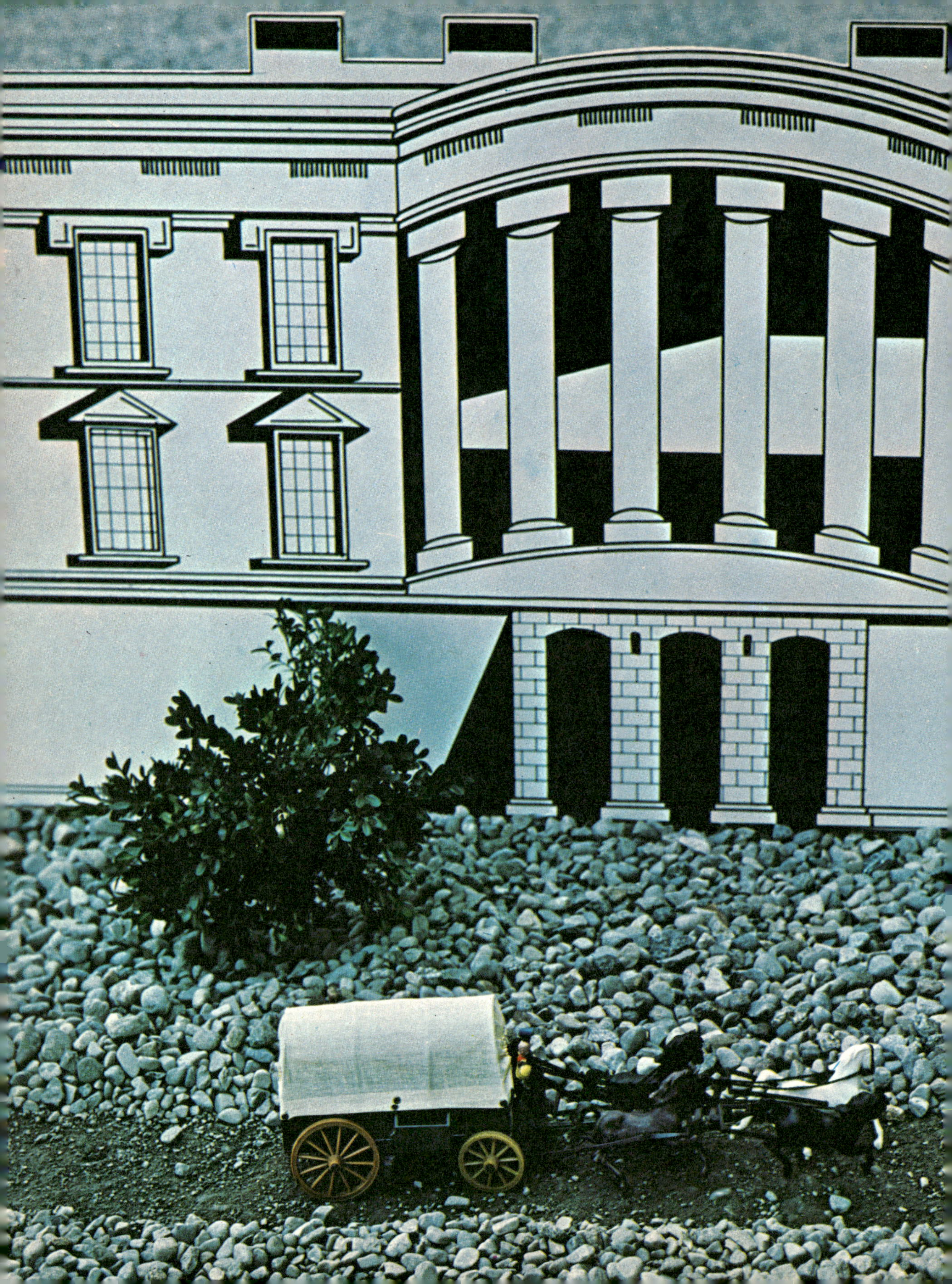

Frontier lands

The covered wagon is shown on a rocky road in front of the White House in Washington, D.C. in the United States. Washington in the District of Columbia is the capital city of America (or the United States). The White House is the home and office of the president of the U.S. Washington is on the east coast of America, the area where the first English colonists settled. The covered wagon was the transport for many settlers who took the rough and rocky road from the Atlantic Ocean's east coast to the Pacific Ocean's west coast.

In the nineteenth century, men, women, and children began to go west. Cities on the eastern seaboard (or coast) grew more crowded. So people sought the freedom of more space, free or cheap land, and the right to build a better, healthier life on the frontier. As people settled the frontier lands, pushing the Indians farther west, clearing forests, farming and building towns, new states were carved from the land. These states joined the original thirteen, making the United States bigger and bigger. Slowly the United States grew to become a republic of forty-eight states, until the middle of this century when Hawaii and Alaska finally brought the total up to fifty states.

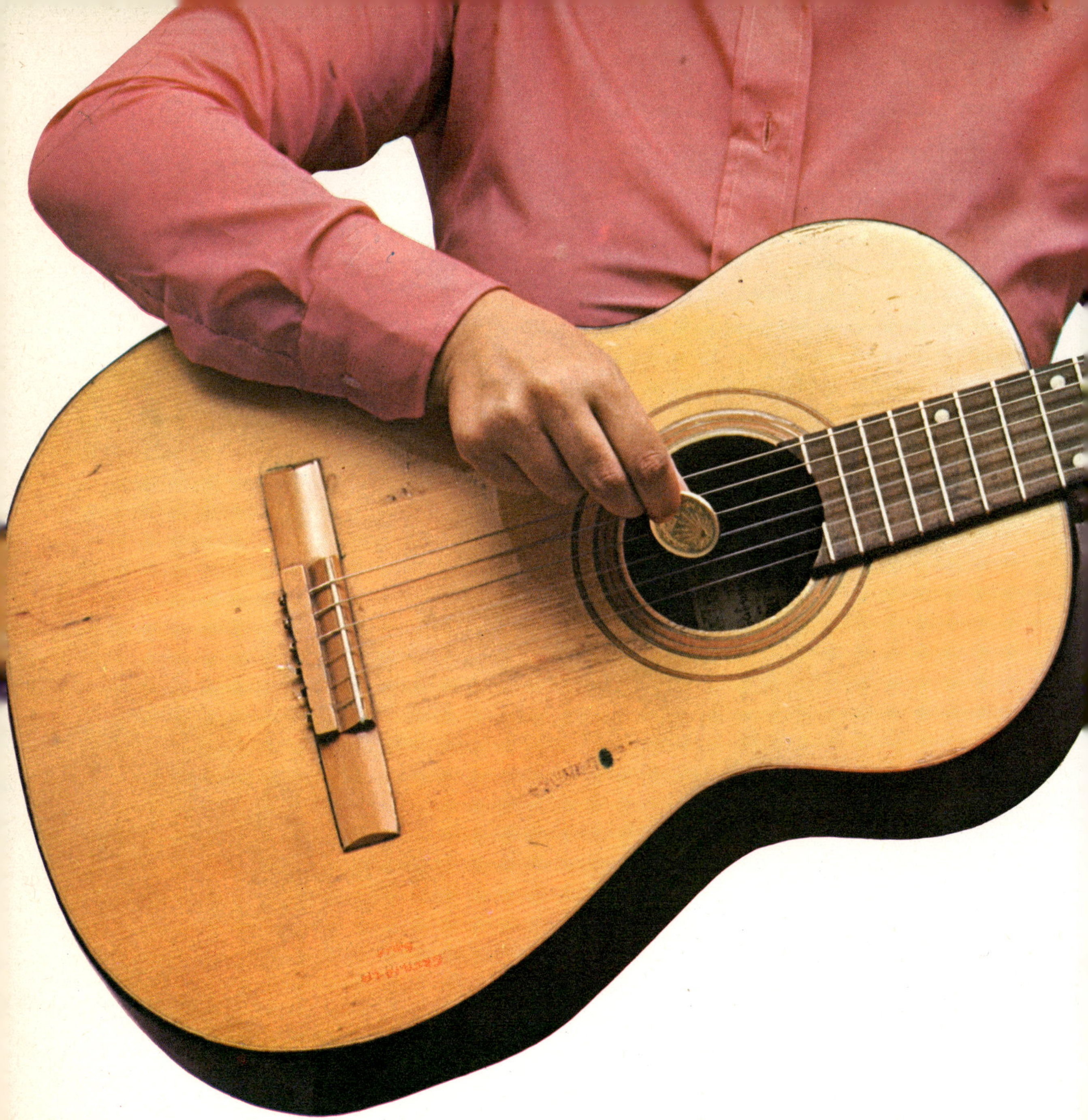

People power

There are many myths and legends about the growth and the settlement of America. Most of us are familiar with the story as seen in films called "westerns". White settlers make the long hard trek west over mountains and across deserts. Cowboys fight Indians, goodies fight baddies. Meanwhile, back at the ranch, the cowboy sits over his guitar strumming and humming "O, give me a home, where the buffalo roam . . ." All these things were true of America, but the country had other problems too.

After gaining their freedom from Britain, the new United States were governed largely by wealthy, aristocratic landowners. New democratic freedoms were needed. Gradually government was organized so that every citizen of the United States could make his individual wishes known by the way he voted. People voted for the most minor government posts like sheriff of a township (which would be the same as a chief constable in a large town in Britain). They voted for men to run each individual state, they voted for president. People voted for individuals, not just political parties, although slowly two main political parties rose to power, the Republicans and the Democrats. Between about 1824 and 1854, Americans worked hard to build a fully free land in which individual men and women could have a real say in government. Great progress was made although many injustices existed still.

Cotton fights brick

The northern and the southern states of America fought a bitter civil war between 1861 and 1865. The southern states owned black slaves and produced cotton. They hated the progressive bustling prosperous way of life in the industrial north.

The two ways of life clashed. When Abraham Lincoln became president of the United States and declared that slavery was "a moral, a social, and a political wrong", one by one the southern states tried to secede from (leave) the United States. So the war was fought to preserve unity and to abolish slavery. The stronger north won.

The growth of industry

America lagged far behind Britain in the growth of industries and factories. Industries often began in a garden shed. They would slowly grow using more workers, selling more goods, and then expanding further. By the time of the Civil War between the north and south, industry was big business in the north. Wheat and grain were big business in the middle of America, and cotton was big business in the southern states.

After the civil war, the machine age boomed in the north and in the west. The south went through a bitter period of poverty and backwardness—for the north did not carry out Abraham Lincoln's plea for "malice towards none and charity for all." The removal of black slavery and the bad treatment from the north made the south an area of radical bitterness. Blacks streamed north into the big cities seeking jobs and a better way of life. The jobs were there, but a better way of life often was not. More than a hundred years after the war, a famous black American political leader would stir his people to a renewed struggle for real freedom in work and in everyday life with the words . . . "I have a dream . . ." His dream was the dream of all Americans —a dream of progress and freedom achieved in peace, a dream of equal prosperity.

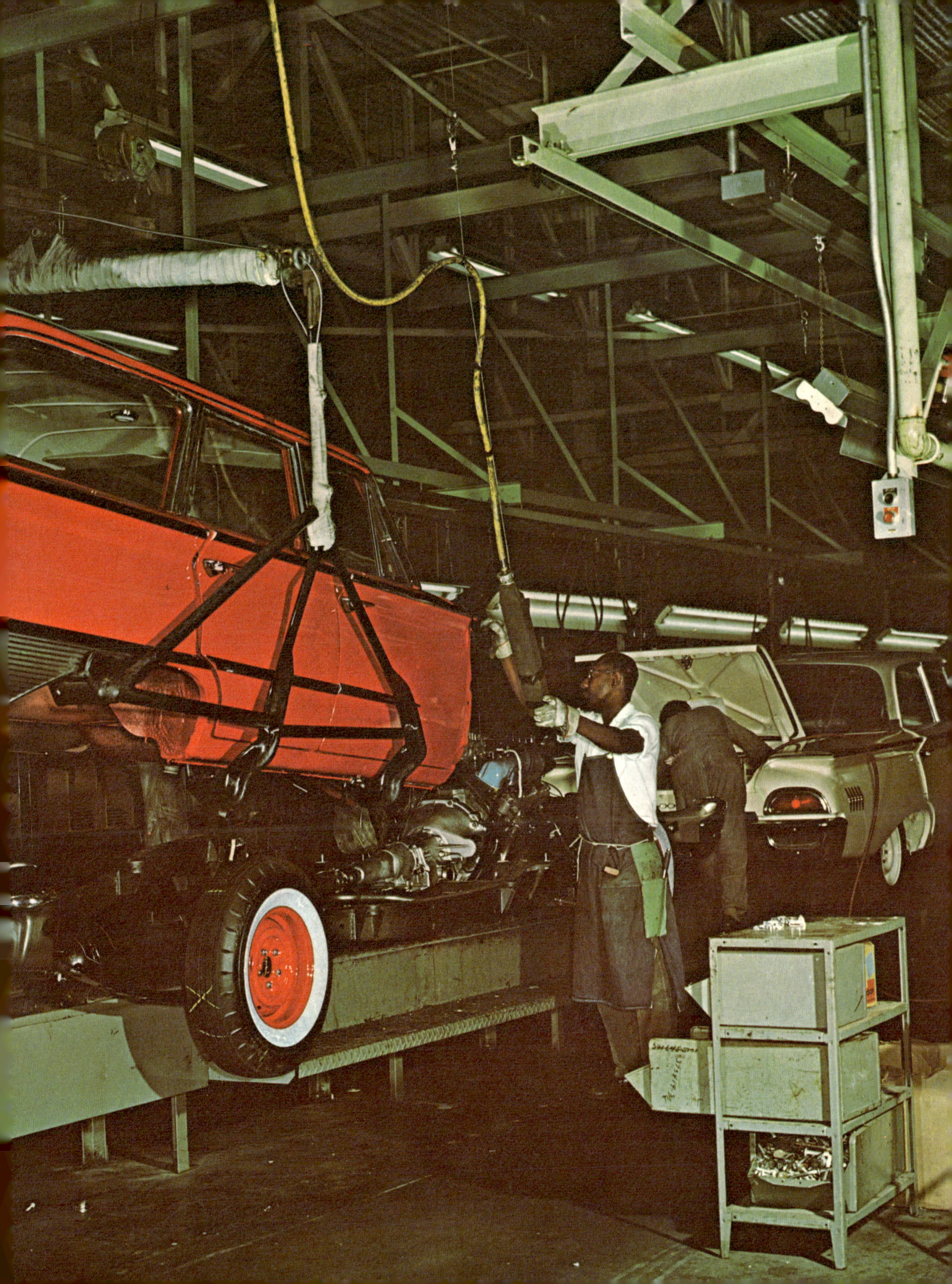

Yearning to be free

In the harbour of New York City stands the famous Statue of Liberty, a gift from the French people to the American people. A plaque on the statue reads: "Give me your tired, your poor, your hungry masses yearning to be free..." America became a dream to many Europeans, for there anyone of any class could achieve a much better, more independent way of life. People (called immigrants) began travelling from European countries to America. At first the British came, then Germans, Scandinavians, Irish, Italians, eastern Europeans (Lithuanians, Russians, Poles, Hungarians), and many others. The flood of immigrants became a tidal wave by 1882 when about 800,000 people travelled with their worldly goods in baskets and bundles to the new world. Slowly the country stopped being a land of small farmers and became much more industrialized. Immigrants went to the cities and found work in factories there. By the end of the nineteenth century, the United States almost equalled the industrial power of Great Britain and Germany combined, in producing goods. A new world power arose, taking its strength from the peoples of Europe who had settled there.

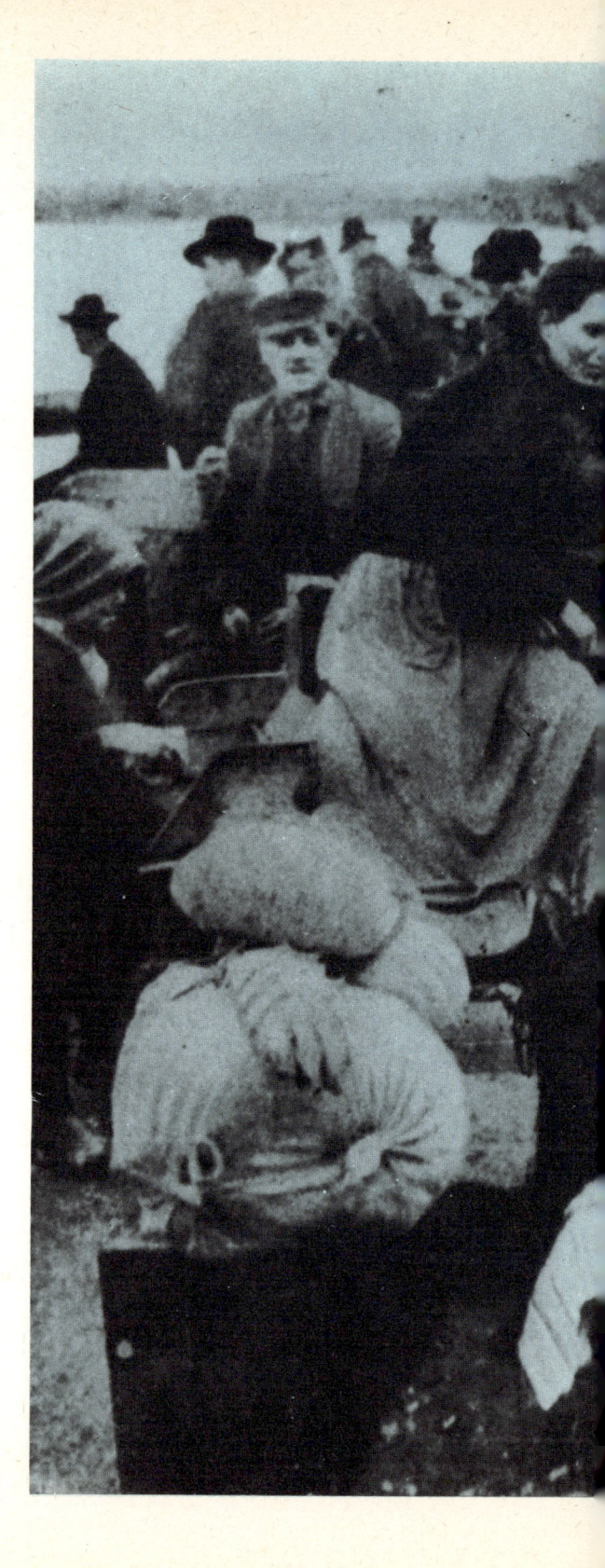

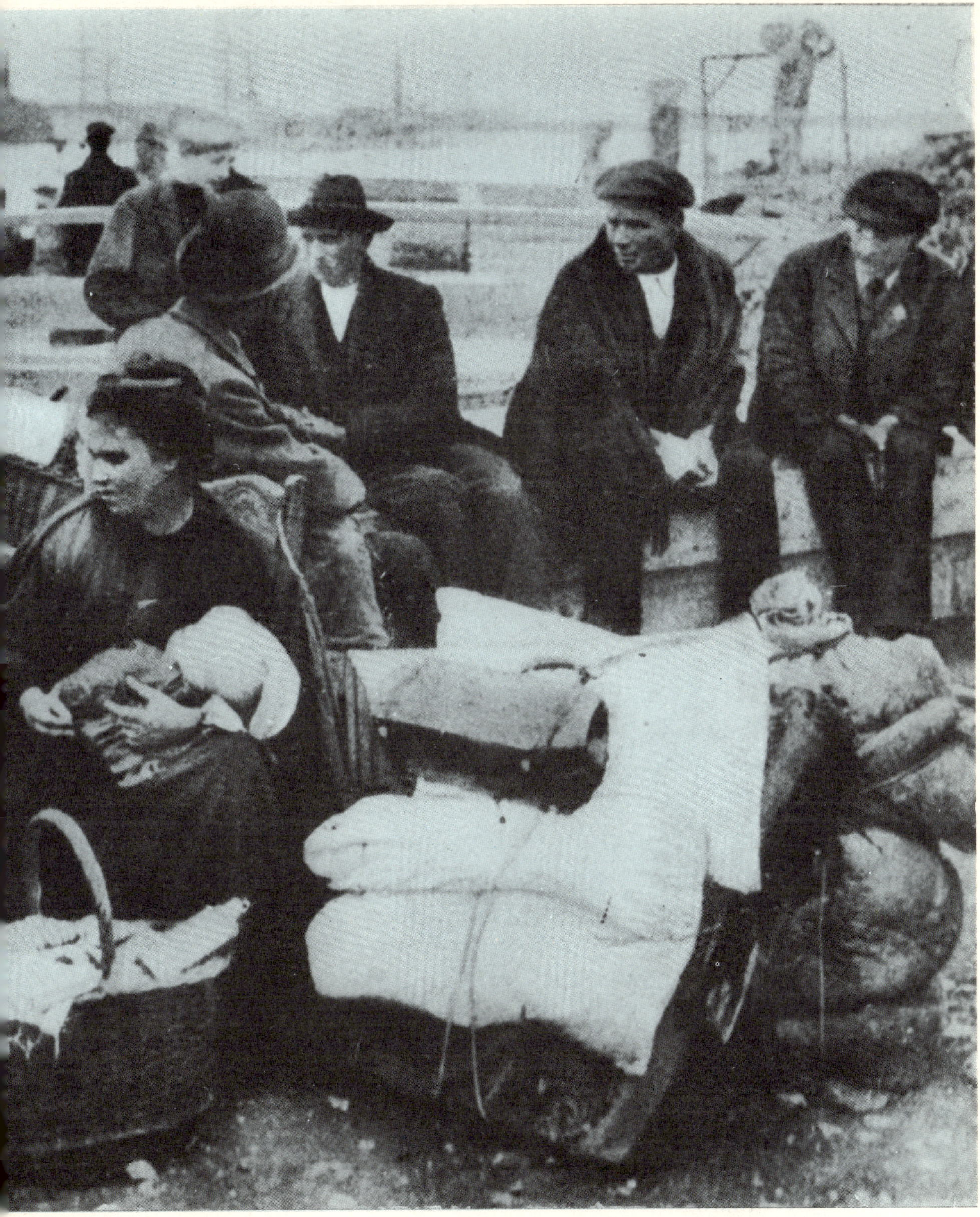

Progress speeds up

From the middle of the nineteenth century, railways were built throughout the world. The railways themselves became faster and more efficient. As transport became easier and better, ideas as well as manufactured goods and food crops travelled farther. Steam-powered ocean-going ships also made journeys faster where railways were impossible.

Now people in one country could learn what people in another country were like and how they lived. As people and nations gained more money, more people had leisure time to find out about people besides themselves. A new social consciousness grew up. This meant that mainly middle class Europeans and Americans began to look around them and see that life for the majority of the world's people was not as safe, secure, or as clean and healthy as it should or could be.

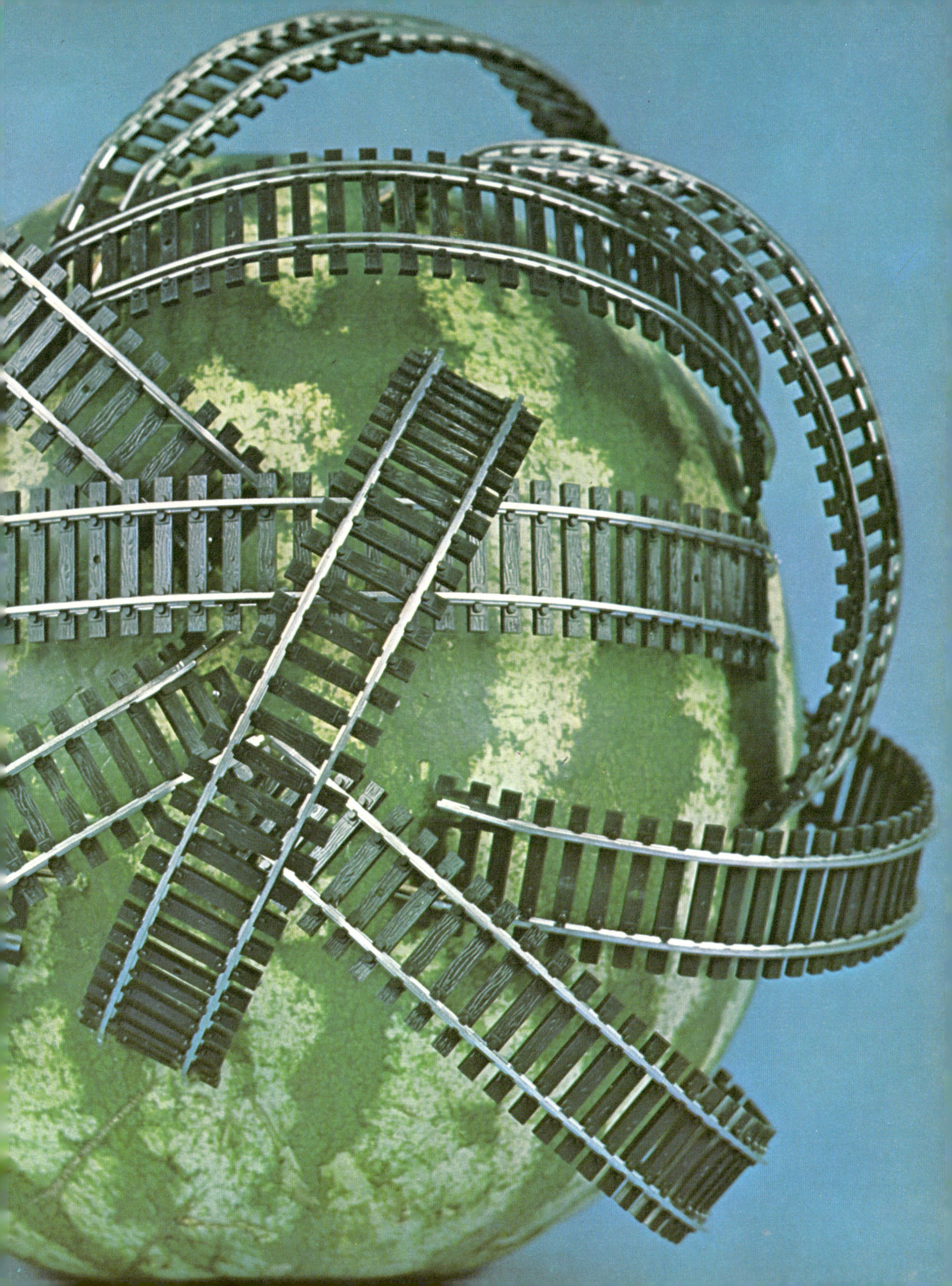

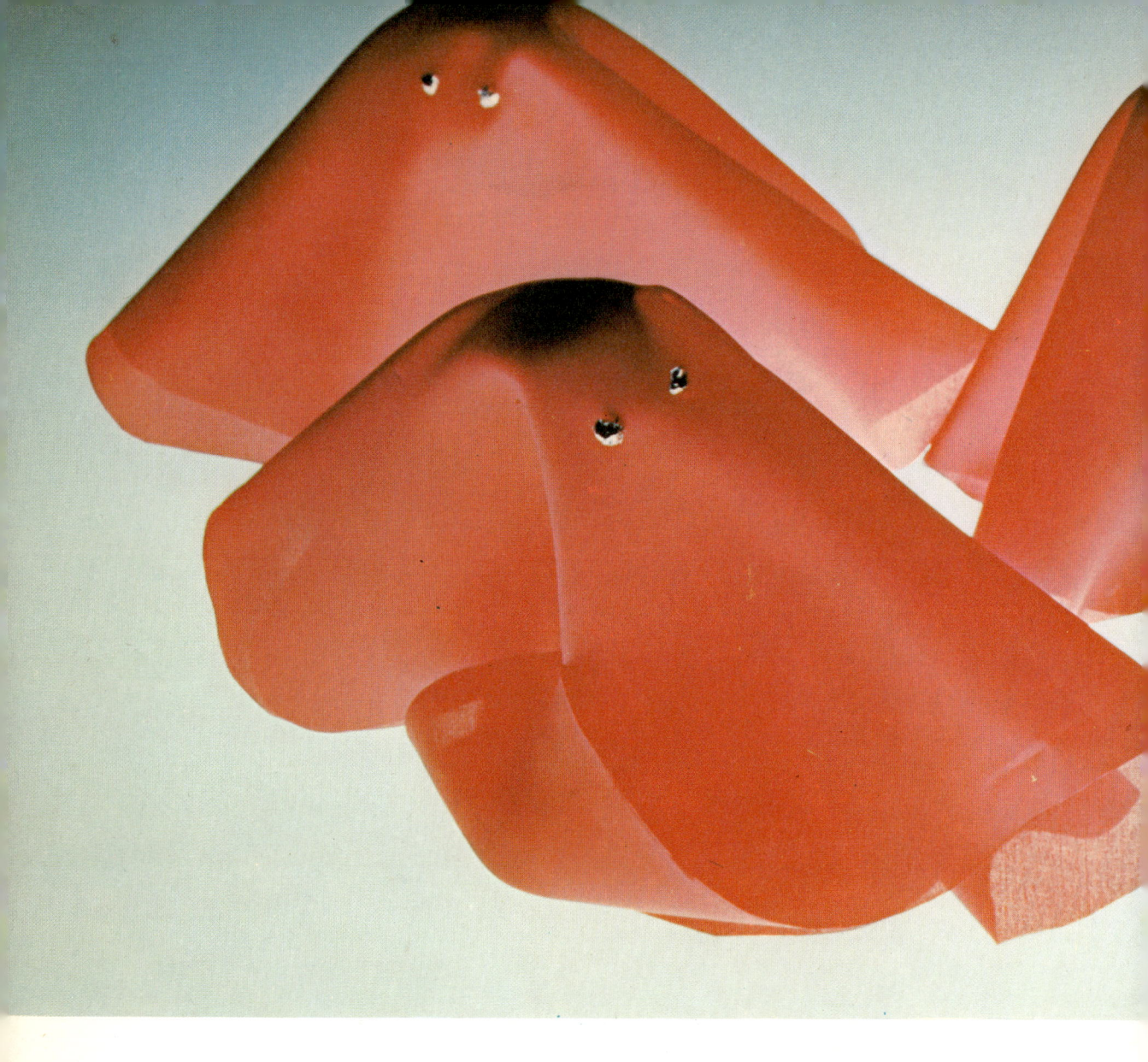

The bogey-man will get you!

Old stories told to children often ended with the words, "And the bogey-man will get you if you don't watch out." This was a kind of ending to a story which would send chills of excitement down children's spines. The bogey-man was a nameless, formless scary creature who was thought to whisk children away in the night from their secure homes.

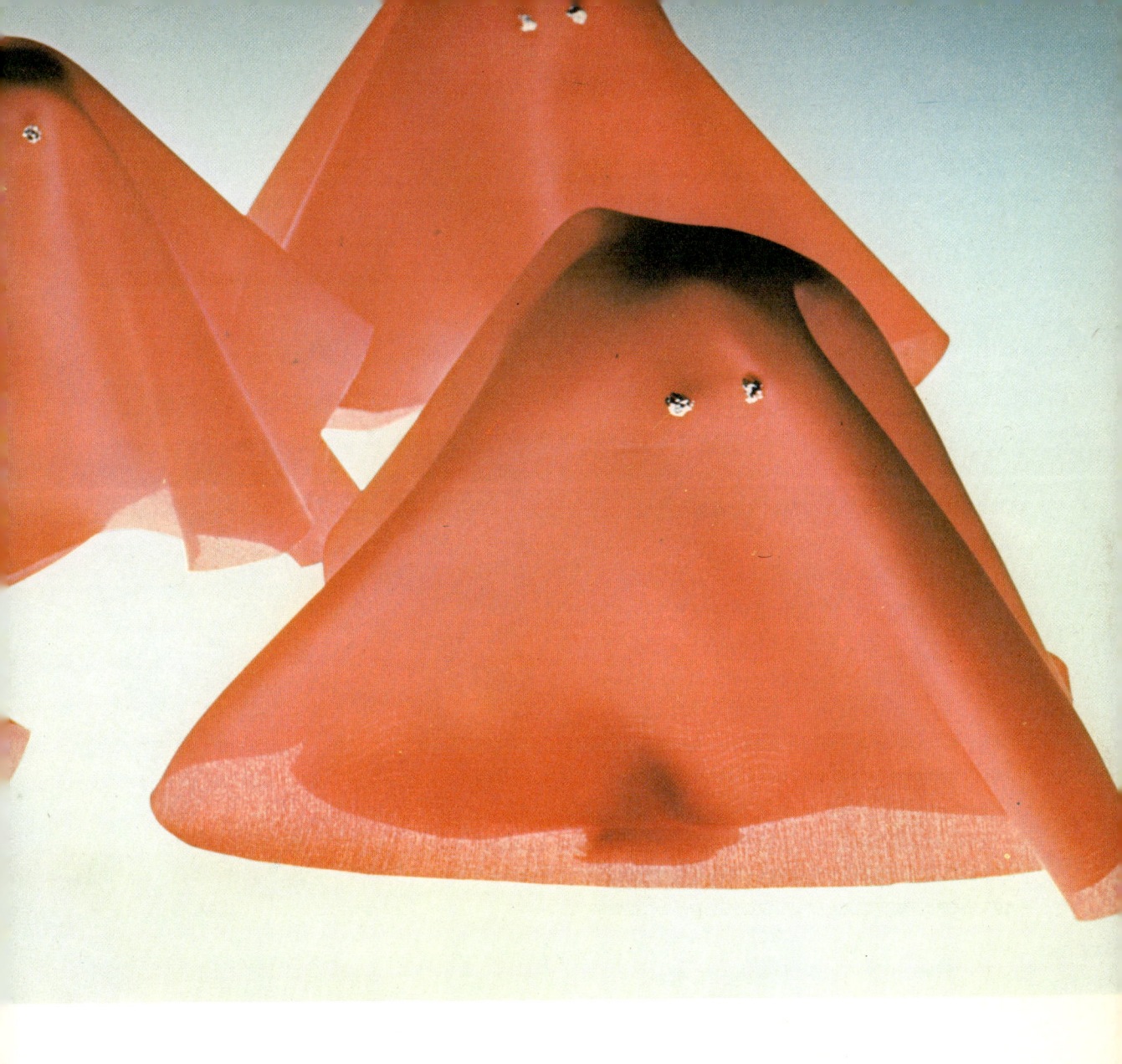

During the nineteenth century and the Industrial Revolution, many adults felt the same kind of scary feeling little children feel about bogey-men. Adults were often unsure of their jobs, scared about whether they would be able to feed their families, and worried about their children's futures. While some progress had been made in giving the masses of people more freedom and more say in government, living conditions were still often terrible.

Children's life

During the early years of the Industrial Revolution, life was very hard for children. Most of them did not play and go to school; they worked. The children of the working class were poorly fed and had few clothes and often no shoes. In the cities, starving, sick, ragamuffins were a common sight. Children had little time for relaxing or enjoying life—as this little boy in the picture is doing.

Slowly a few reforms or changes helped to improve life for children. In 1833 a law called the Factory Act came into being in Britain: it laid down that children under eighteen could not work more than eleven and a half hours a day, and children under twelve could only work eight hours in textile or cloth-making factories. After 1842 it was unlawful to employ boys under ten in coal mines. Slowly employers began to realize how wrong it was to work little children for long hours, or to beat them if they did not work hard enough.

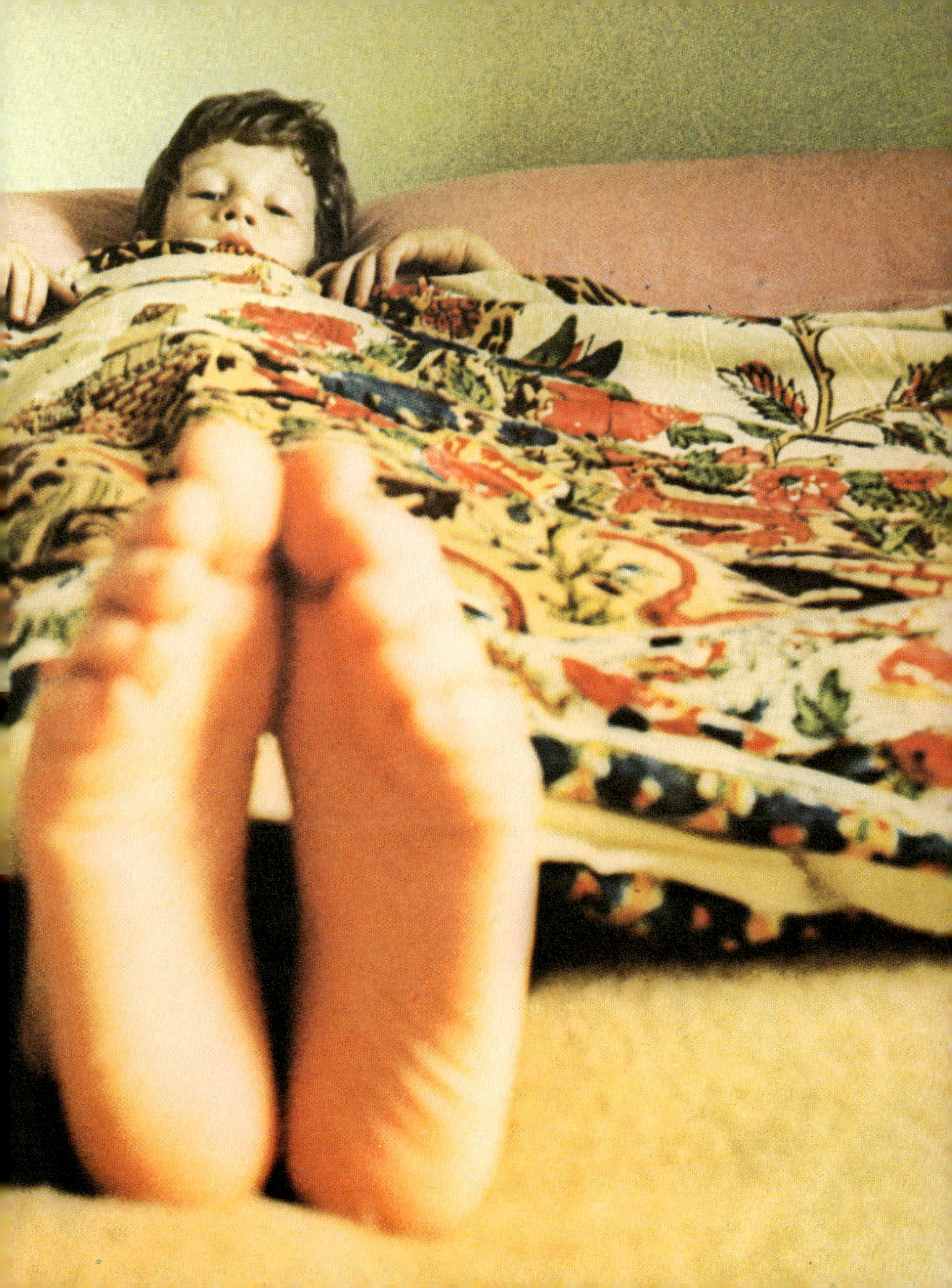

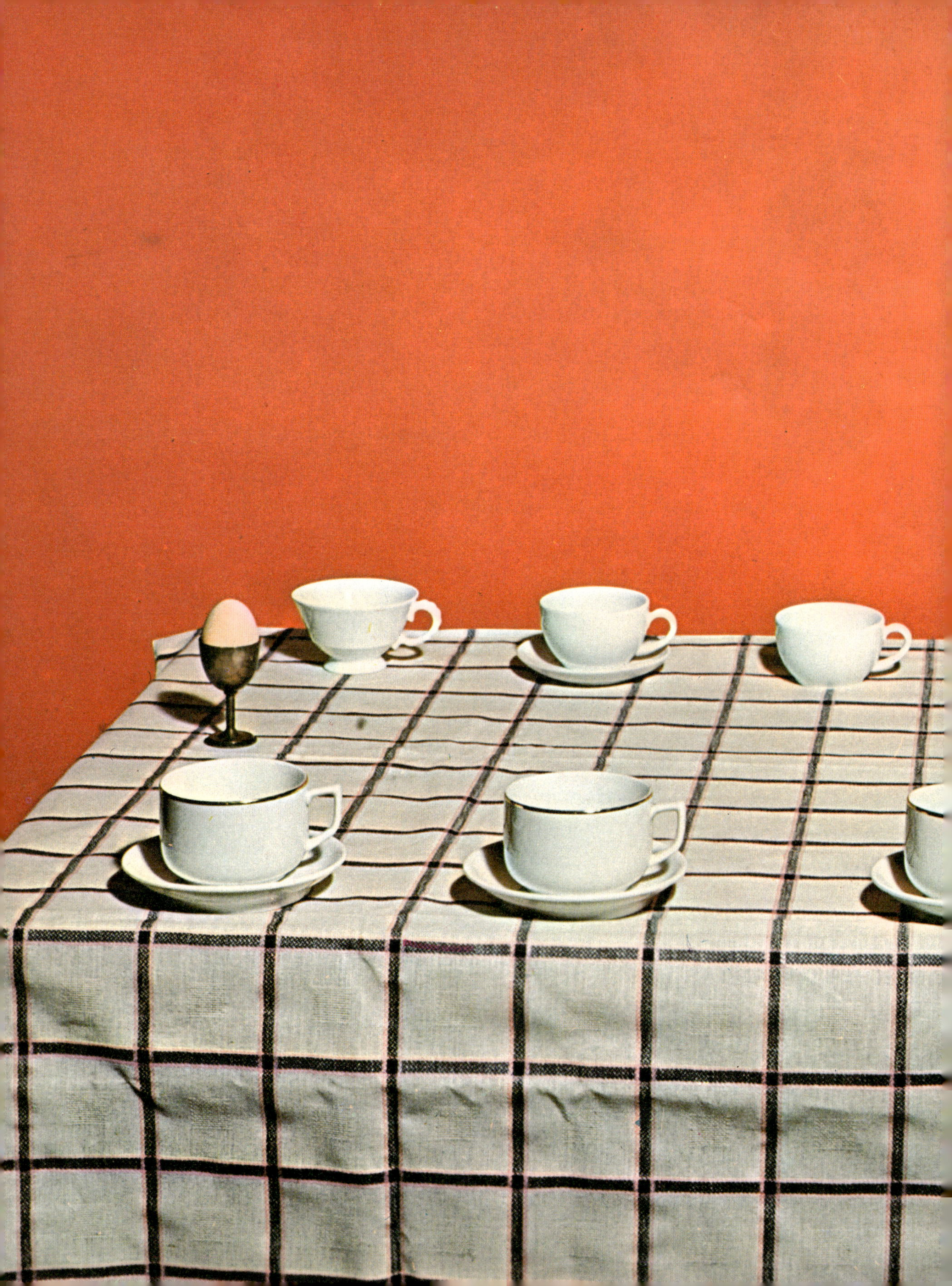

The table of society

In the nineteenth century, despite the very hard living conditions for masses of people, individual men and women all felt they had a place in working towards a better kind of society. The cups and eggcups on the table show that whatever their class or background they had a right to share together in the new material progress. Certainly the aristocracy (or old noblemen) still had special privileges and silver eggcups. The middle class ran big business and had big china cups with silver rims. The working class might have china tea cups or earthenware cups, but they were working and fighting for a better society too.

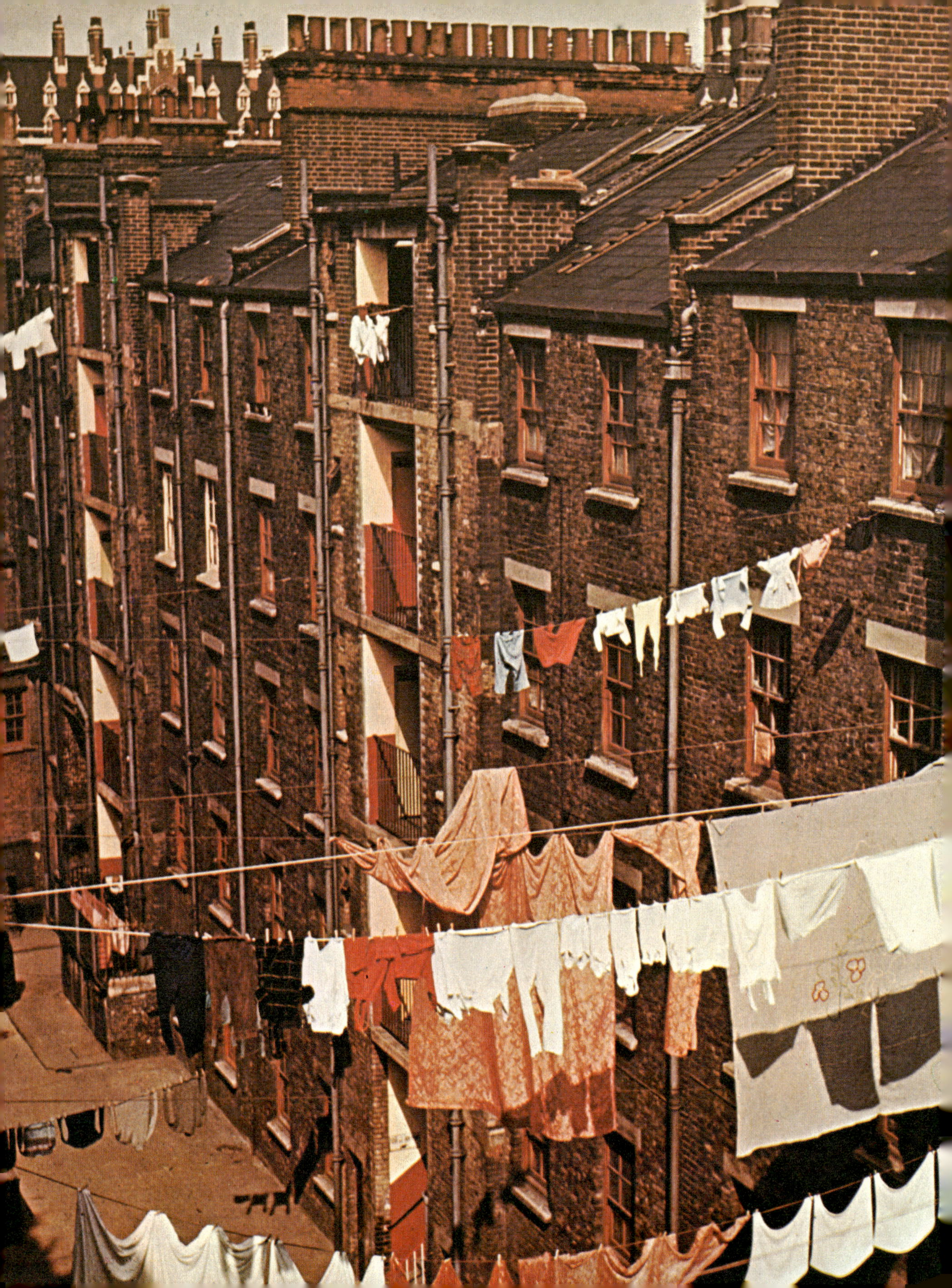

Slums of progress

By the 1870s and the 1880s, people began to realize that there was a horrible as well as a hopeful side to the progress of the Industrial Revolution. The big cities were not beautiful places of freedom and hope for the masses of people. They were the scene of slums—large areas of cheap and nasty housing where too many people lived in too few rooms. Much of the slum housing had been put up in haste, to house the workers who were streaming from the countryside to find work in factories. In the slums, crime and disease flourished side by side.

Many reforms were made law in these years—long overdue laws. A Public Health Act was passed in Britain which led to healthier food and attempts to make the streets and housing cleaner. Working men were given the right to form trade unions to bargain for better working conditions. There were attempts to clean up and clear away slums. Education for children was made compulsory. Children now had to attend school for a certain number of years.

Clean and healthy

For centuries in European towns, cities, and villages, unhealthy and unclean living conditions were common. No one thought very much about being too clean. Nor did anyone realize that being clean helped a person to stay healthy. Try to imagine what the streets of an old-fashioned village were like. People dumped chamber pots onto the street, and threw away rotting food in the gutters. These gutters were the same down which rain water flowed—to the village's central water well. At the well, women washed clothes, people drank, and drew up buckets of water for drinking and washing.

In the nineteenth century, men of science discovered that germs breed disease and sickness. They also discovered that germs flourish and multiply in filthy conditions. Great discoveries were made about the conditions which caused many diseases. As scientists learned more about being clean and leading healthy lives, there were attempts to make public life cleaner, and to make people aware of how important it was to be really clean and to live in clean houses.

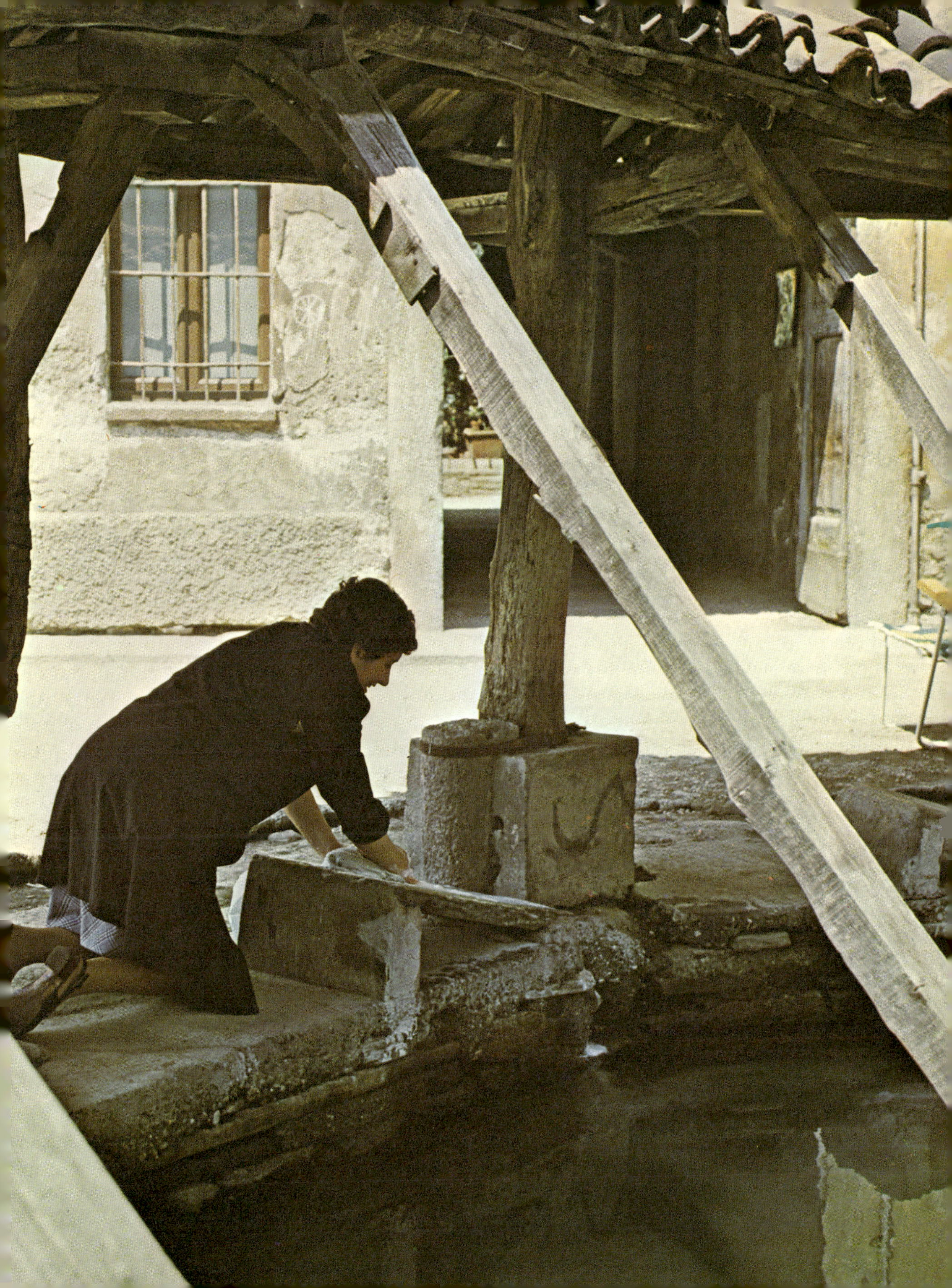

Crime and punishment

For centuries, prison was a threat which hung over the heads of whole families. The most minor of crimes—stealing a crust of bread to keep from starving, for example—were punished in harsh and cruel ways. Whole families were sent to prison if their father could not pay a small debt. People were imprisoned for their political views, and for publishing books and pamphlets. Prisons were horrible places; rats crawled about the floor, lice infested clothing and hair, food was abominable. People grew sick and died with no care at all. Little children were locked up with adults, abused by the prison guards. The people locked up in prisons were full of misery and despair and hatred towards the society that could treat them so brutally. Slowly towards the end of the nineteenth century, there were prison reforms. Punishments became less severe. Torture was outlawed. Some medical care was provided when people were ill.

Photograph: Mary Evans Picture Library

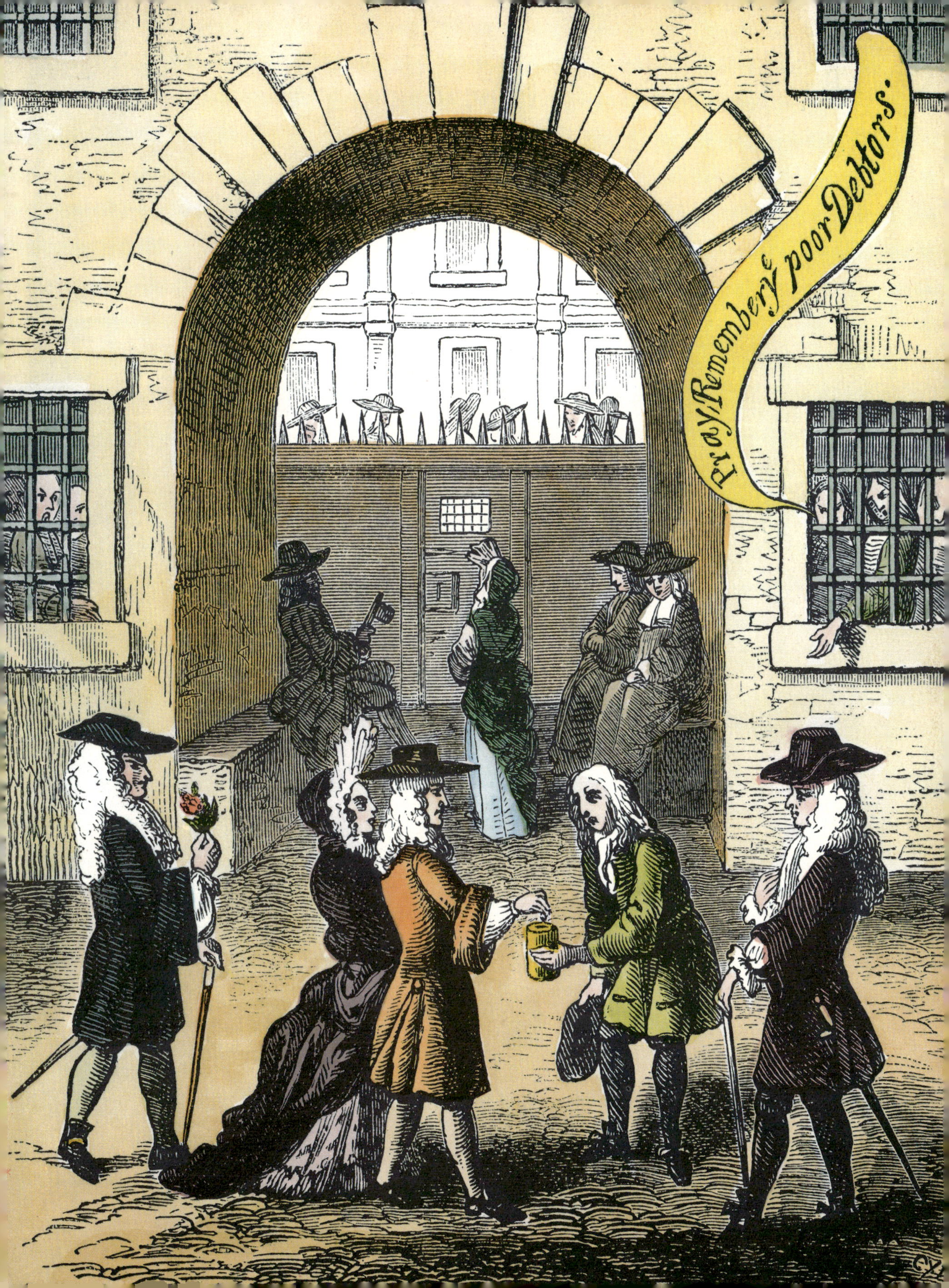
Pray Remember ye poor Debtors.

A new luxury

From the middle of the nineteenth century, a new luxury began to brighten people's lives. This was an increase in leisure time, and a little spare money to spend on entertainment. Soon there was more public entertainment for the mass of the people.

Brass bands played for the public's enjoyment in parks, and paraded in the streets. Organized games like football and cricket were played for the public's enjoyment. Churches organized sports teams and there were family picnics and outings. People even travelled on railways to go to the seaside for short holidays.

The specialist

A specialist is a person who is expert in doing one particular kind of activity or work. The picture shows a highly skilled craftsman at work—a diamond cutter. To be an expert in his work, the diamond cutter needs to use his own judgment and intelligence, to have years of experience, and to be able to work with expensive and complicated machinery. No ordinary unskilled workman can do his job.

By the 1880s the boom in business and industry required more and more skilled men and women and more specialists. The kinds and types of work available were much more varied and required more education and training. Primary or first education for children was more or less available to everybody in Europe and in America. Now higher education was needed. Technical schools and classes were started to teach older children and adults more skilled work. Academies, institutes, colleges, and universities were set up to teach everything from advanced methods of farming to the new engineering skills.

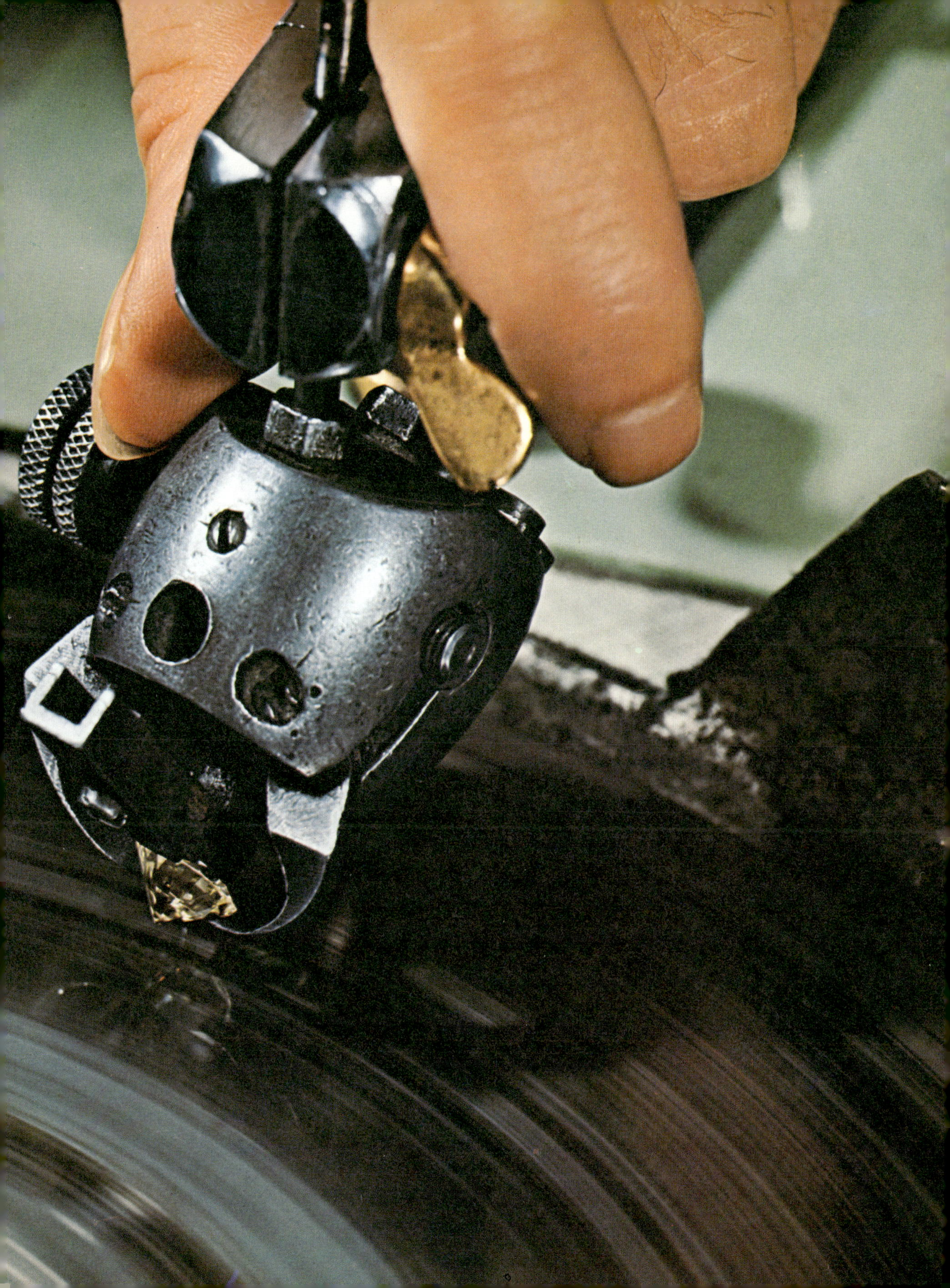

PHYSICIANS RECOMMEND THE "WILSONIA" MAGNETIC

CORSETS AND WAISTS FOR DAY OR NIGHT WEAR

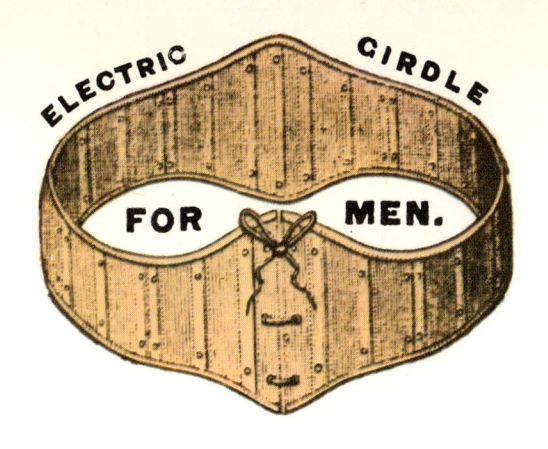

Scientific magic

The discovery of electric current and the harnessing of electric power are perhaps the most useful of all scientific inventions. Once the power of electricity was understood, invention followed invention. People began to believe that electricity could do anything. It was like a new scientific magic. Practical and useful things were powered by electricity—indoor and outdoor lights, the telephone, the telegraph, big machines in factories.

Electricity was so exciting to people in the nineteenth century that many not-so-useful electrical things were made and sold to the public. The old-fashioned advertisement pictures show you some of the goods people used to be able to buy: electric hair brushes, electric corsets for ladies and electric girdles for men. The advertisements suggest that people believed electricity to be some kind of "magic power", good for everything. Can you think of some funny or not-so-very useful electrical things people buy today? Just how useful do you really think an electric toothbrush is? or electric hair curlers?

Man studies mankind

From the middle of the nineteenth century, science took a new and exciting turn. Scientists began to try to study the human being scientifically. They no longer just observed man's physical movements. They tried to understand how the body worked inside and out. They began to try to think scientifically about where man actually came from and who his real ancestors were.

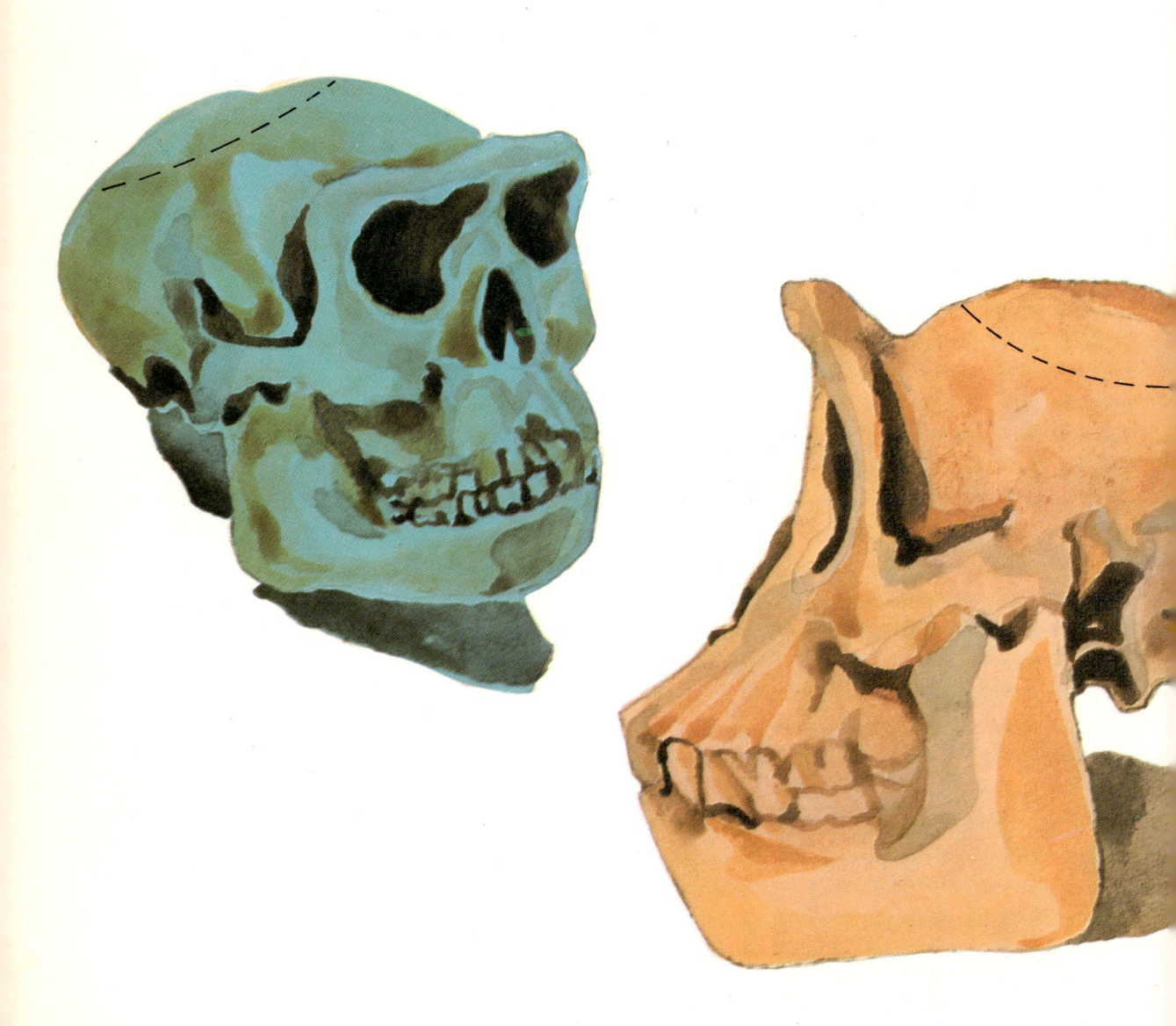

They began to study the brain, and to try to study what went on in the brain. Before the end of the century, a new kind of scientist was at work—the psychologist. He would try to understand just what went on inside man's brain.

The new scientific study of mankind began with the publication of a book in 1859 which shocked people far and wide. This was *On The Origin of Species* by Charles Darwin. This Englishman proved to be the scientific genius of the century. He suggested that man was descended from the apes. He believed this could be proved by observing both apes and man scientifically. Darwin's book outraged many, many people for they believed God had made man in his own image, and God was surely not an ape.

Survival of the fittest

Charles Darwin wrote another book called *The Descent of Man*. This time he concentrated on the idea that each person's special characteristics are inherited (passed on) from his parents, grandparents and so on, right back through all his ancestors.

The ideas of Darwin and of a French biologist Louis Pasteur inspired others to study ways of making people healthier. Darwin suggested that in nature it is only the strongest and fittest animals which survive. And this was true also of human beings, especially at a time when there were many diseases to which they might fall victim.

Pasteur studied germs and diseases. Work based on his findings has made it possible to control, cure, and even prevent fatal diseases spread by germs. Pasteur himself had learned a lot from Edward Jenner, an English physician. In 1796 Jenner had discovered how to vaccinate people against the killer disease smallpox by injecting a tiny dose of smallpox germs into the bloodstream.

Vaccination is successful because, if you have even a very mild attack of a disease (not even enough to make you ill), your body builds up a resistance to the disease. So you have a better chance of staying healthy.

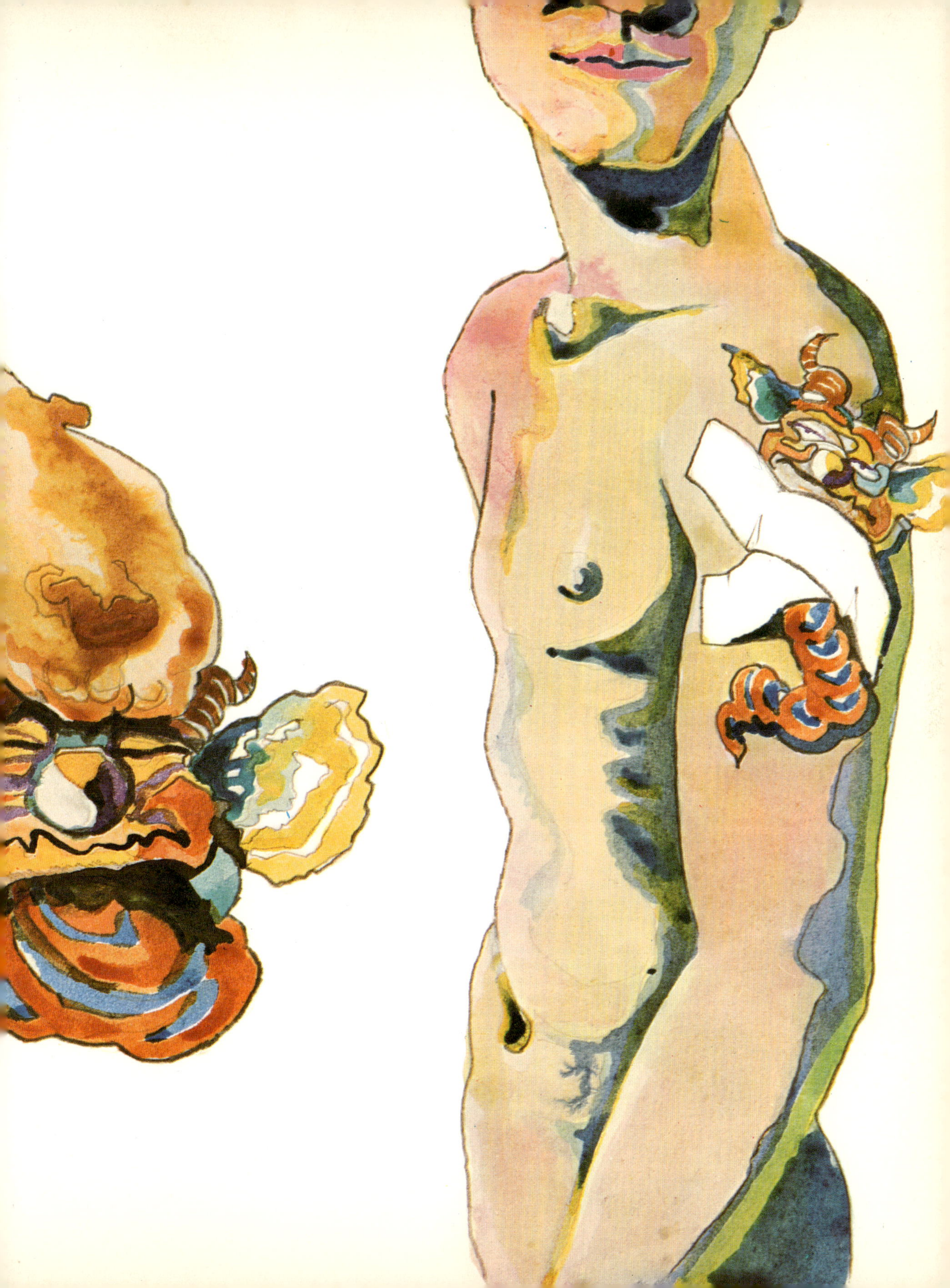

Free or muzzled?

By the end of the nineteenth century, more ordinary people in the world were freer than they had been for centuries. Not everyone was free to speak or to do as he wished, but great progress had been made. People felt hopeful about progress in science, ways of earning a living and conditions of everyday life. The mass of people were no longer muzzled. Dogs are sometimes muzzled so that they cannot bite people. In many countries, people had yet to raise their voices and demand a fairer treatment, but they were growing towards a sense that it was possible. They began to speak their thoughts. People felt that in the new century, the twentieth century, life was bound to be better than ever before.

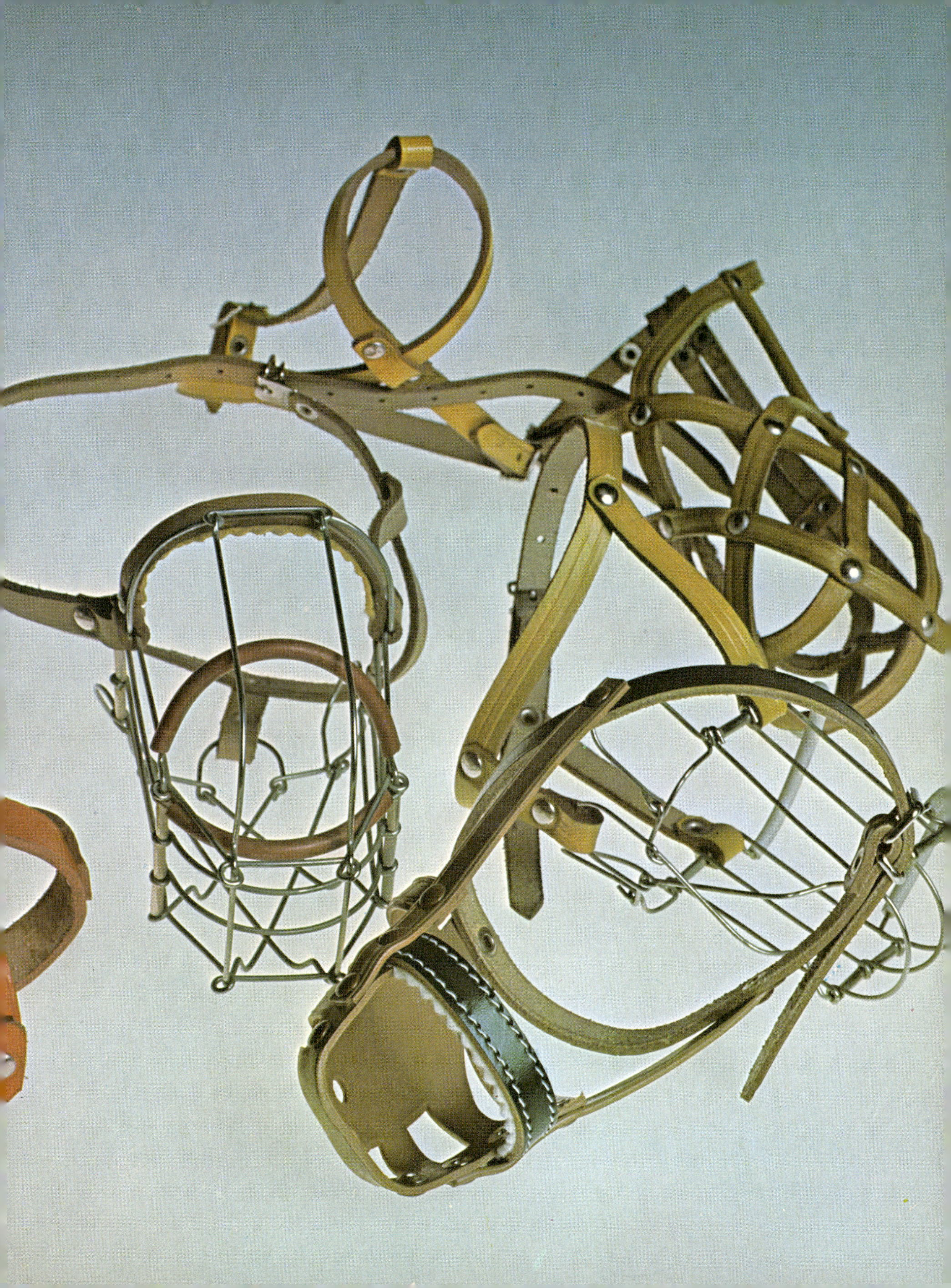

Climb aboard!

Gradually the idea of co-operation began to spread and gain support. Some people saw that everybody could go along together towards a common destination—but, of course, they had to want to.

These ideas were especially important in connection with social questions. Many things could only be done if people would co-operate; so laws were passed which made living conditions better for people who could not afford to pay for things like medical aid. Some attempts were made to provide people with job security—having some measure of assurance that they would not suddenly lose their jobs and have no way of earning a living to support themselves and their families.

These early moves towards what we now call a welfare state did not achieve much, but they were a start. They did show that if you can carry people with you, you can reach your goal more quickly.

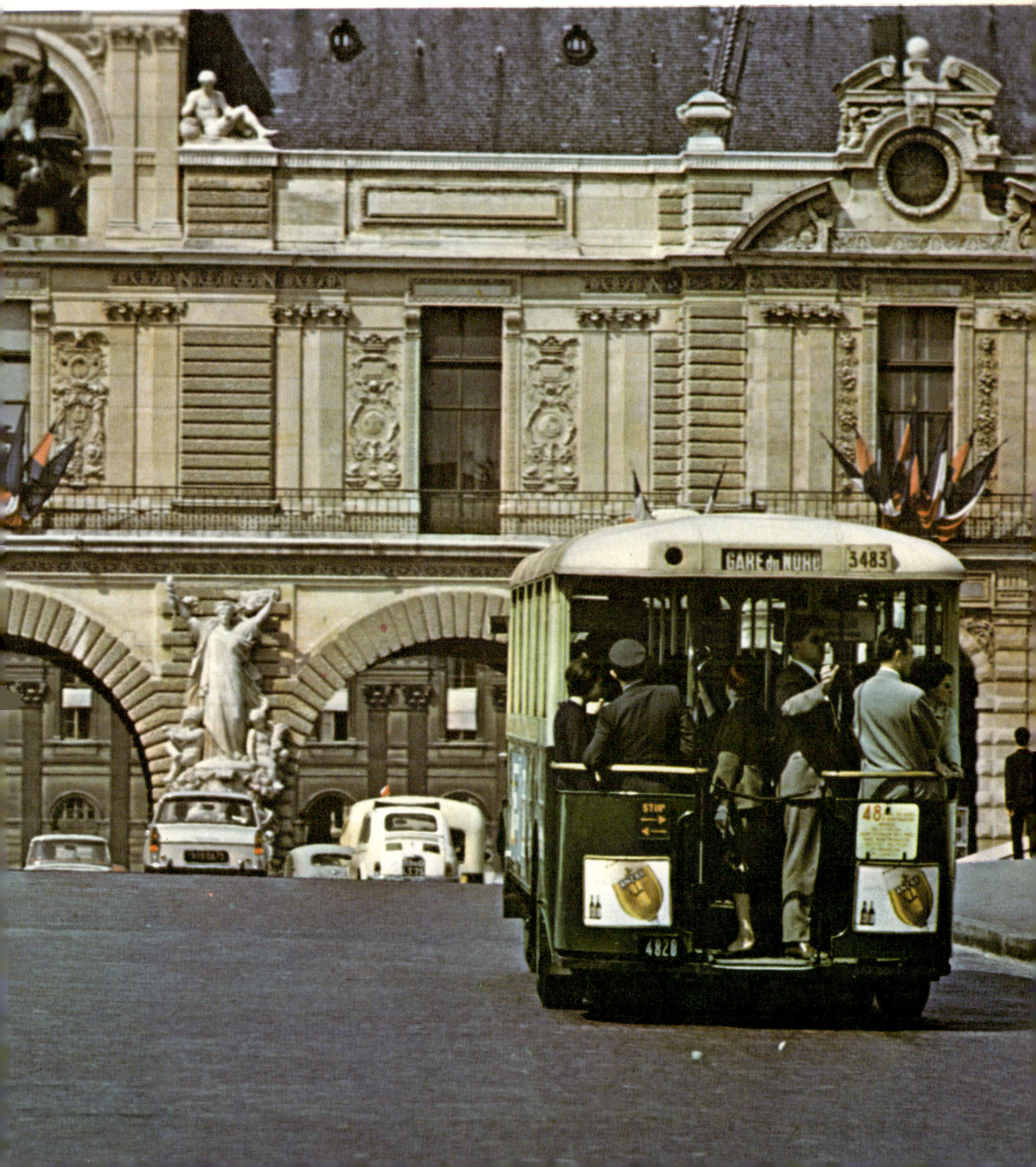
GARE du NORD
3483
STOP
48
4820

Carried on the tide

There was not much emigration from Britain to North America in the 18th century, so most of the people living in Britain's colonies there had made their own way of life and had developed their own customs and beliefs. It was not surprising, therefore, that feelings of anger and resentment towards Britain would build up until there would be no holding back the tidal wave of change.

The arrangements between Britain and these North American colonies were designed to work completely to Britain's advantage, especially in trade matters. And the colonies had to pay for British troops to "protect" them.

The famous Boston Tea Party was one of the events that triggered off the American Revolution, which is also called the American War of Independence. A group of colonists dumped a large cargo of tea into Boston Harbour in protest against yet another tax which had just been imposed on them. Fighting broke out between the rebels, led by George Washington, and British troops. Many bitter struggles followed until independence was declared on 4th July 1776, and the foundations were laid of the United States of America.

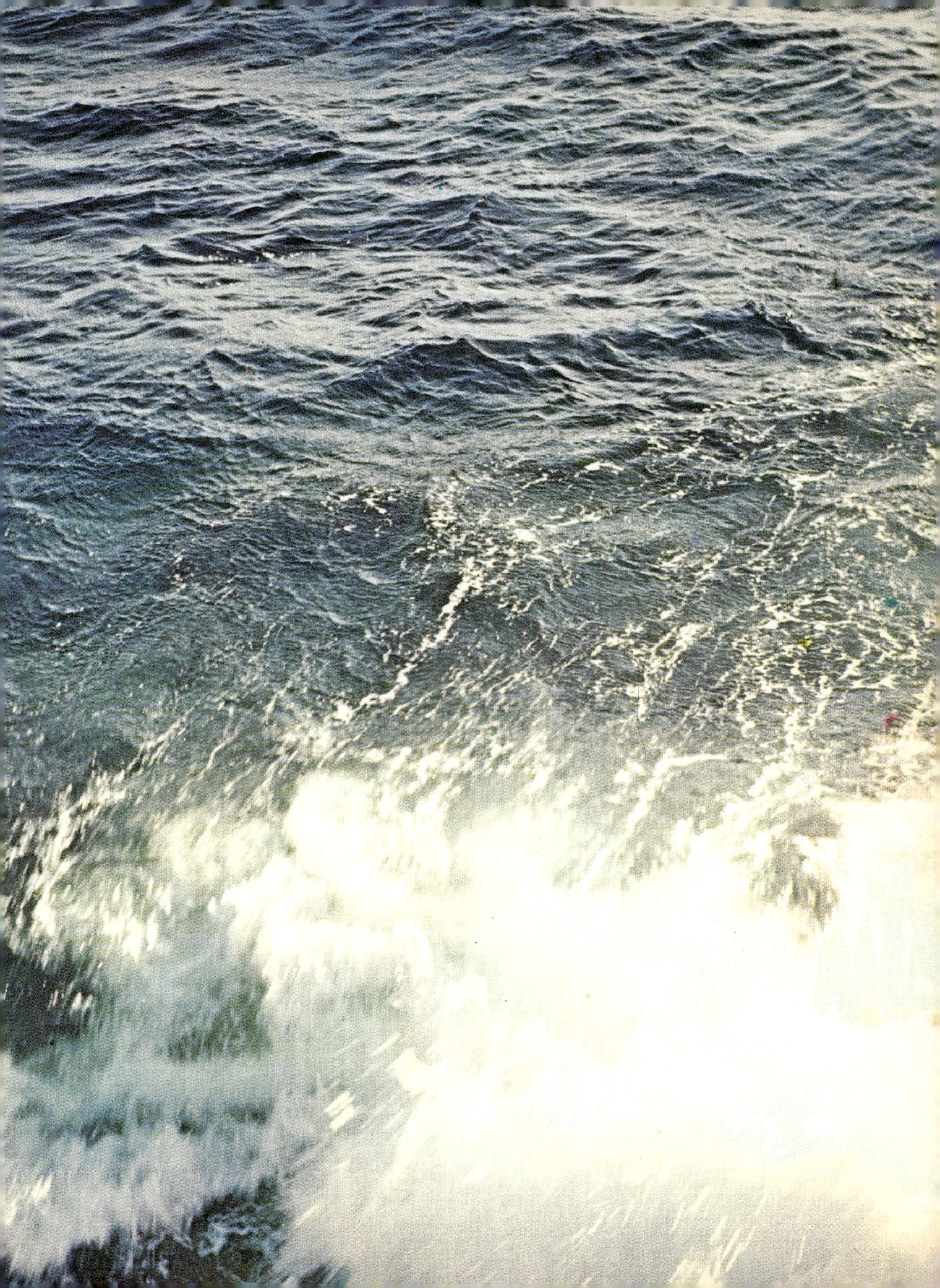

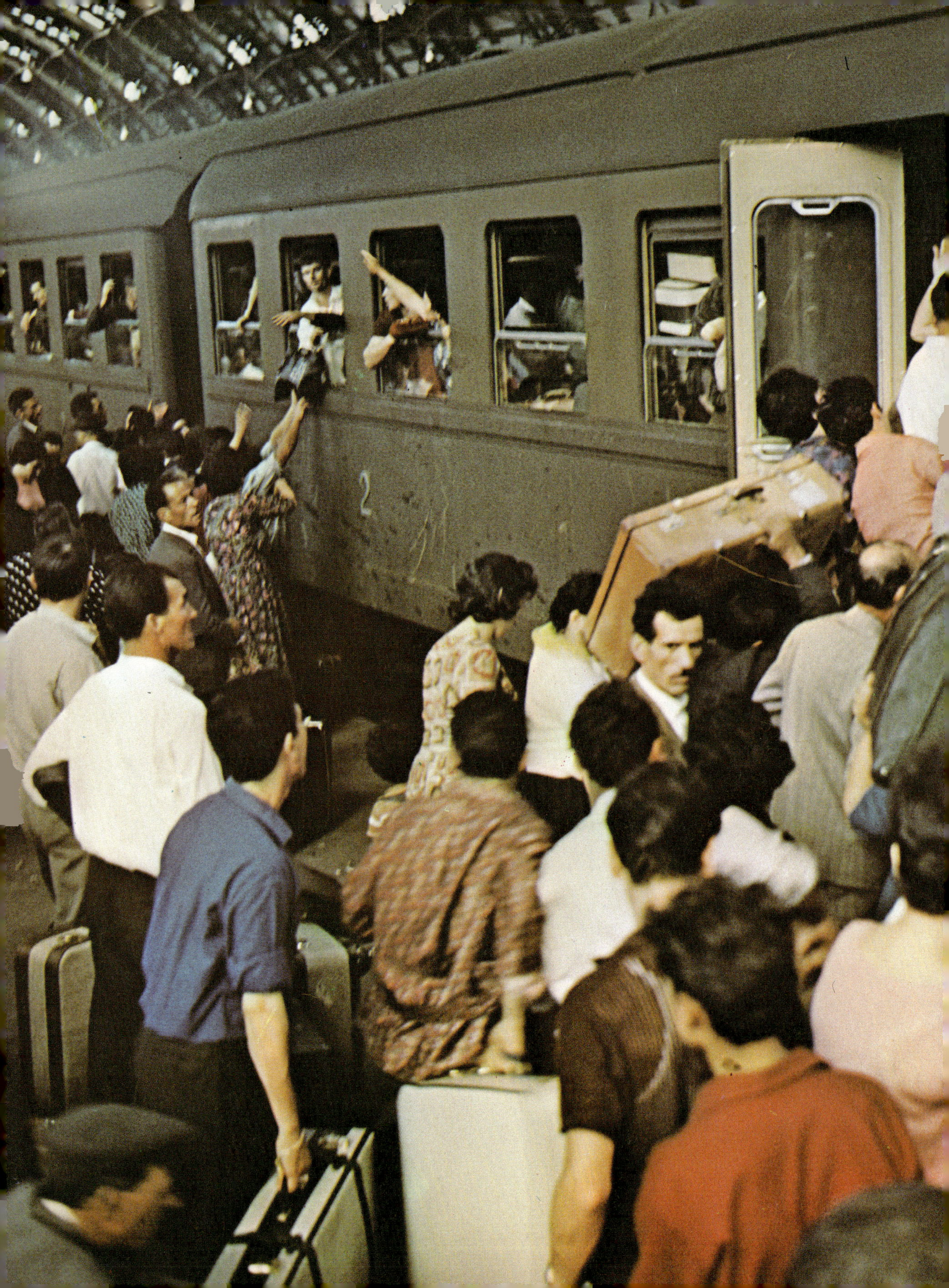

The Gravy Train

When people "jump on the gravy train", we mean they know or think something good is happening, and want to have part of it for themselves.

In Europe in the nineteenth century, there were many fast and exciting developments, there were large fortunes to be made, and there were territories to be taken over. Many people and many nations wanted to get on that gravy train. There was a great rush to make money, to expand.

Large parts of Africa and Asia were acquired (taken over) by European countries. Britain, France and Germany were the main rivals to grab bits of foreign lands to add to their empires. Holland, Italy, Portugal, Russia and Japan were on the gravy train too.

European countries wanted new markets for all the goods they were making with their new machines. They also wanted new sources of food for their increasing populations, minerals for their industries, and of course more and more power and influence in the world.

Britons round the world

The British were the most successful in gaining control over foreign lands. By the end of the nineteenth century, people said that "the sun never set on the British Empire". In other words, the British controlled lands all the way round the world.

Canada in North America, Australia, New Zealand, New Guinea, India and large parts of Africa all became part of the British Empire. Queen Victoria, the reigning monarch of Great Britain, became the Empress of India. During her reign (1837–1901), Victoria saw remarkable progress in all areas of life. The empire brought the Victorian Age to all corners of the globe.

New subjects

As British power spread across the world, many different areas of land became subject to the British crown. Chinese, Arabs, North American Indians, Africans, and Indians became subjects of the British Queen Victoria.

Men and women from England, Scotland, Wales and Ireland, travelled to foreign lands. Sometimes they went for short stays to become part of new businesses or to work for the British government. Sometimes they went to make their homes in the new territories or the new colonies.

Spreading civilization

Wherever people from Europe went in the world, they tried to bring their own familiar way of life with them. The Dutch and the Germans, the French and the British, the Belgians, Portuguese, Spanish, and Italians all brought their languages and customs to different parts of the world. The European nations like Great Britain believed in "civilizing" the "backward" countries. European white men tried to make life in Asia and in Africa as much like life in Europe as possible. As the bottom picture is a pale imitation of the top, so the life Europeans made in their colonies was a pale imitation of life back home.

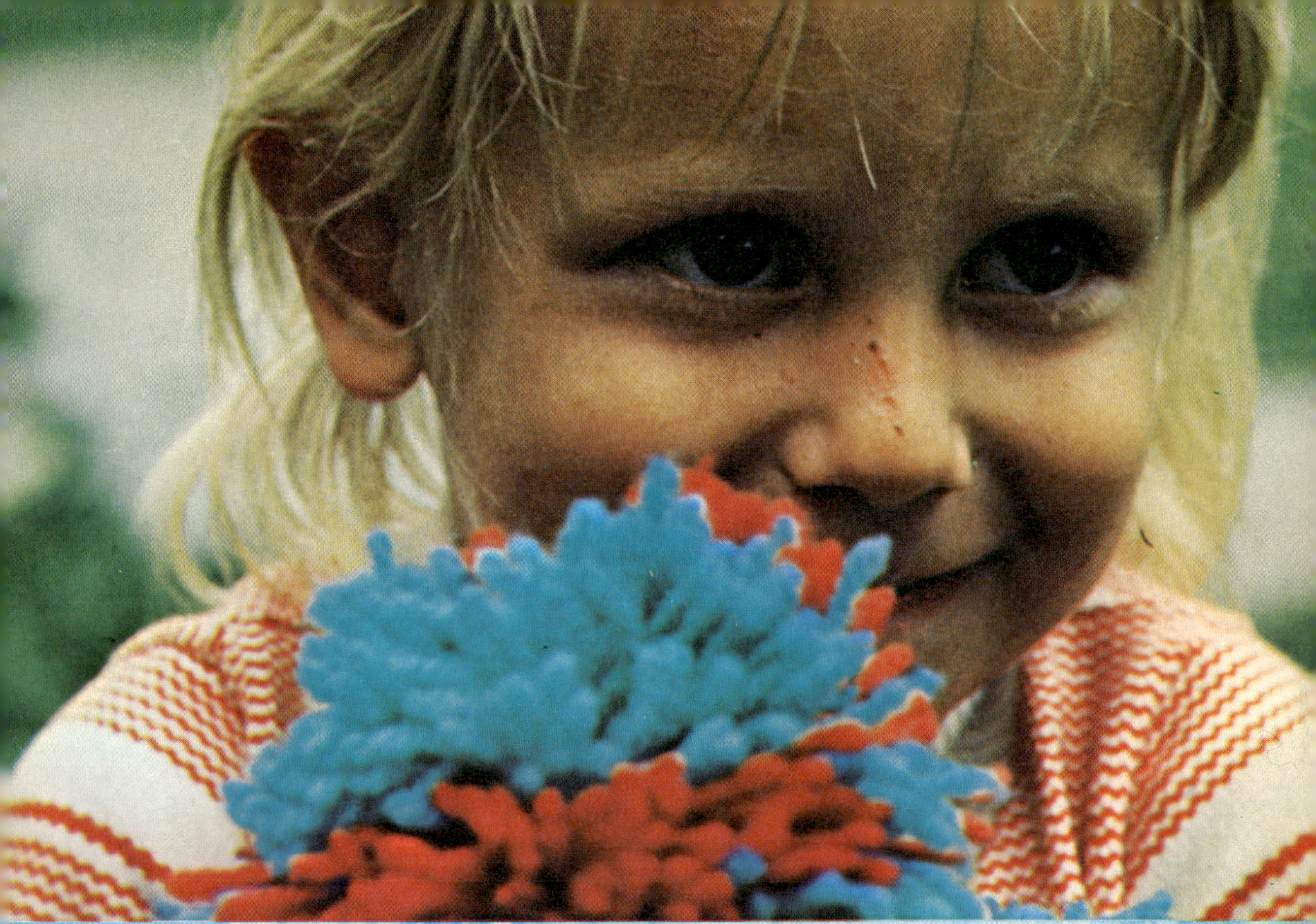
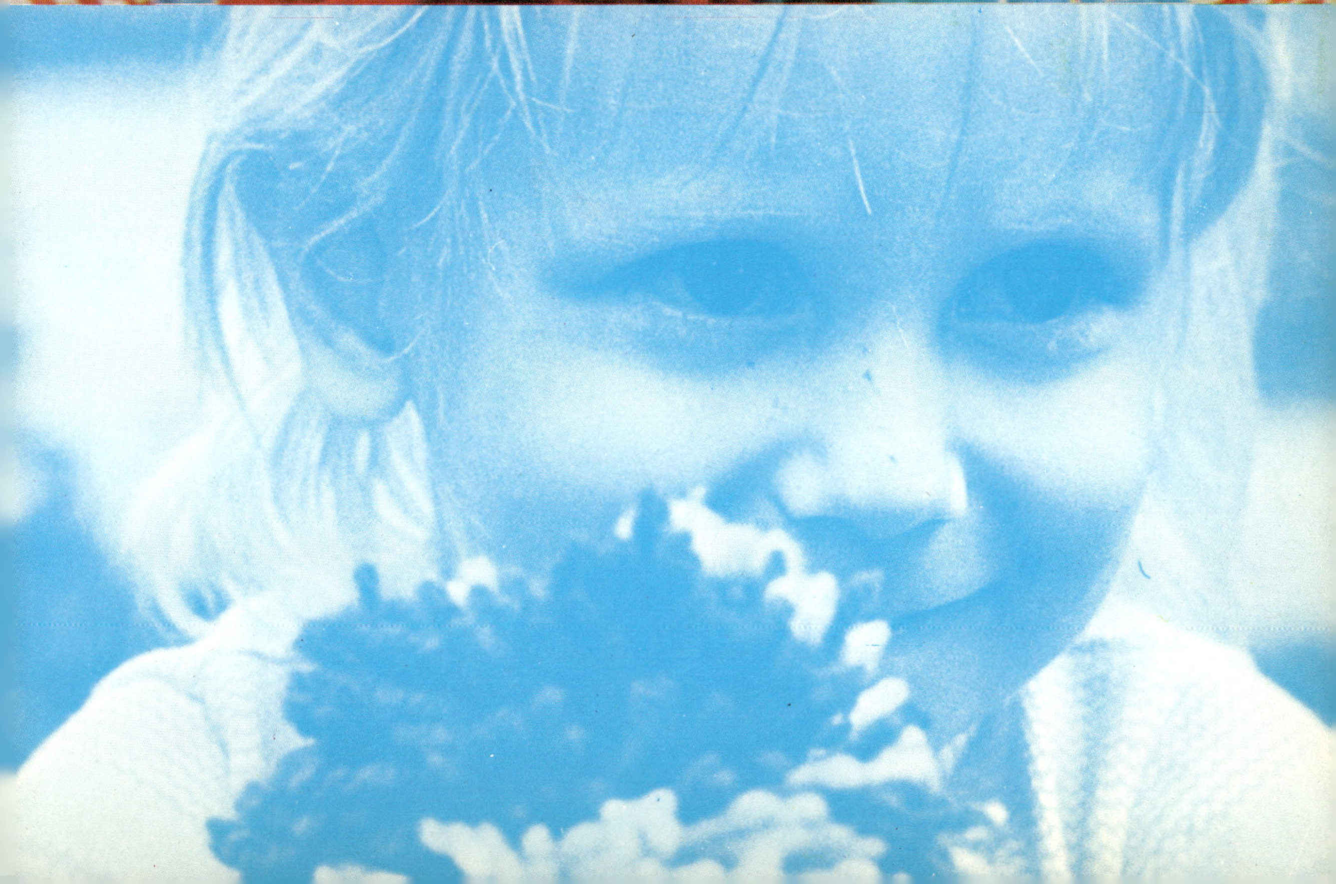

Guns and goods

The spread of European empires across the world went hand in hand with conflict. The rival European powers built railways in their new territories. They built telegraph wires. They sent steamships back and forth with all the precious new raw materials they found in their overseas possessions. Diamonds, gold, rubber, tin, bananas, dates, spices, cocoa, tea, sugar, and many other goods flowed into Europe from all over the world.

There was great competition among the countries of Europe for control over areas of land in Africa and in the east. There was also competition among settlers who had gone out from Europe to make new lives. The natives of the lands which Europeans wanted to control and settle in were often not very happy about having their land taken from them or their crops and precious stones and minerals shipped or exported to Europe. Many battles and even wars were fought. Europeans fought Europeans for control; and Europeans fought native peoples for control.

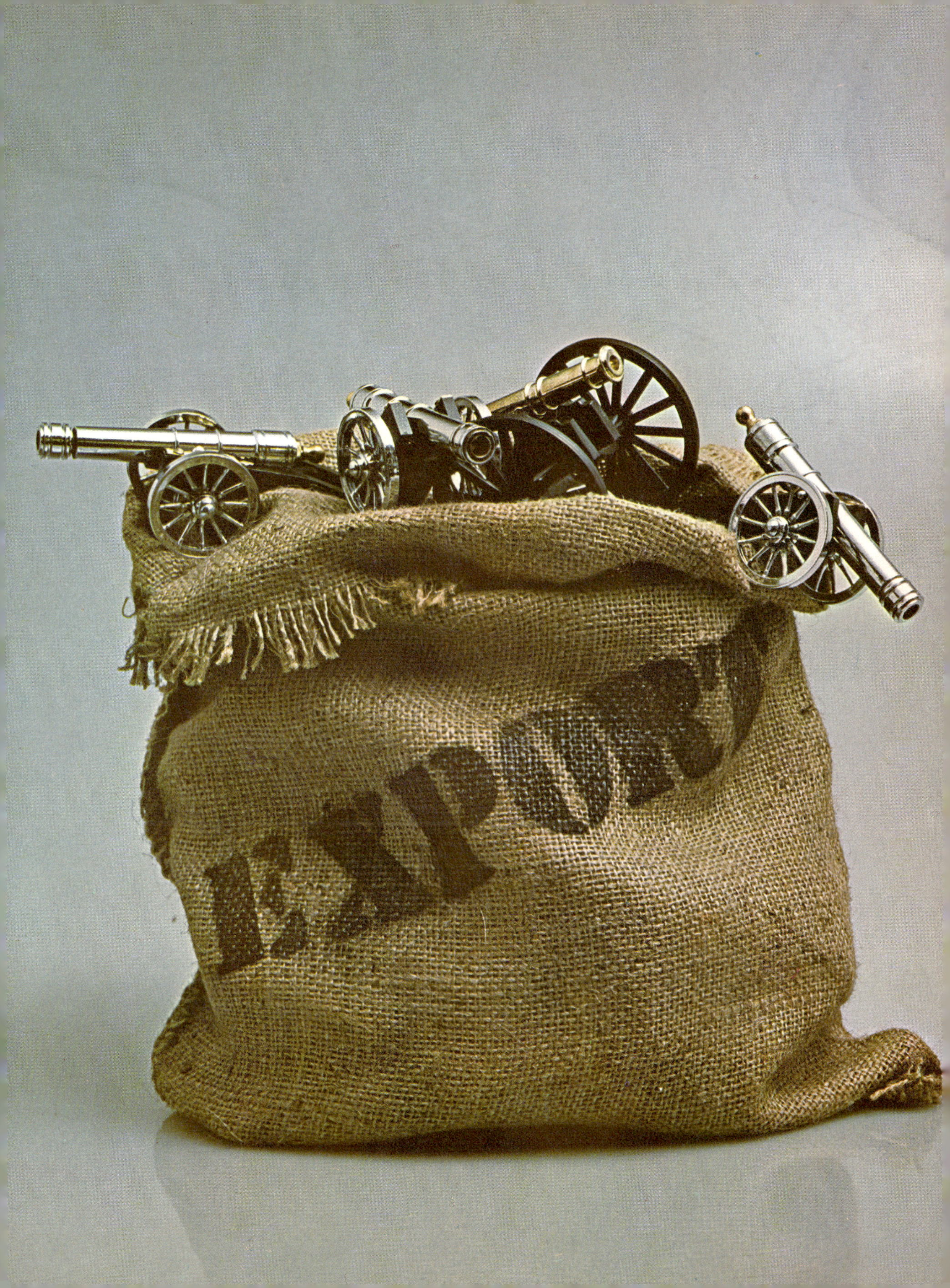
EXPORT

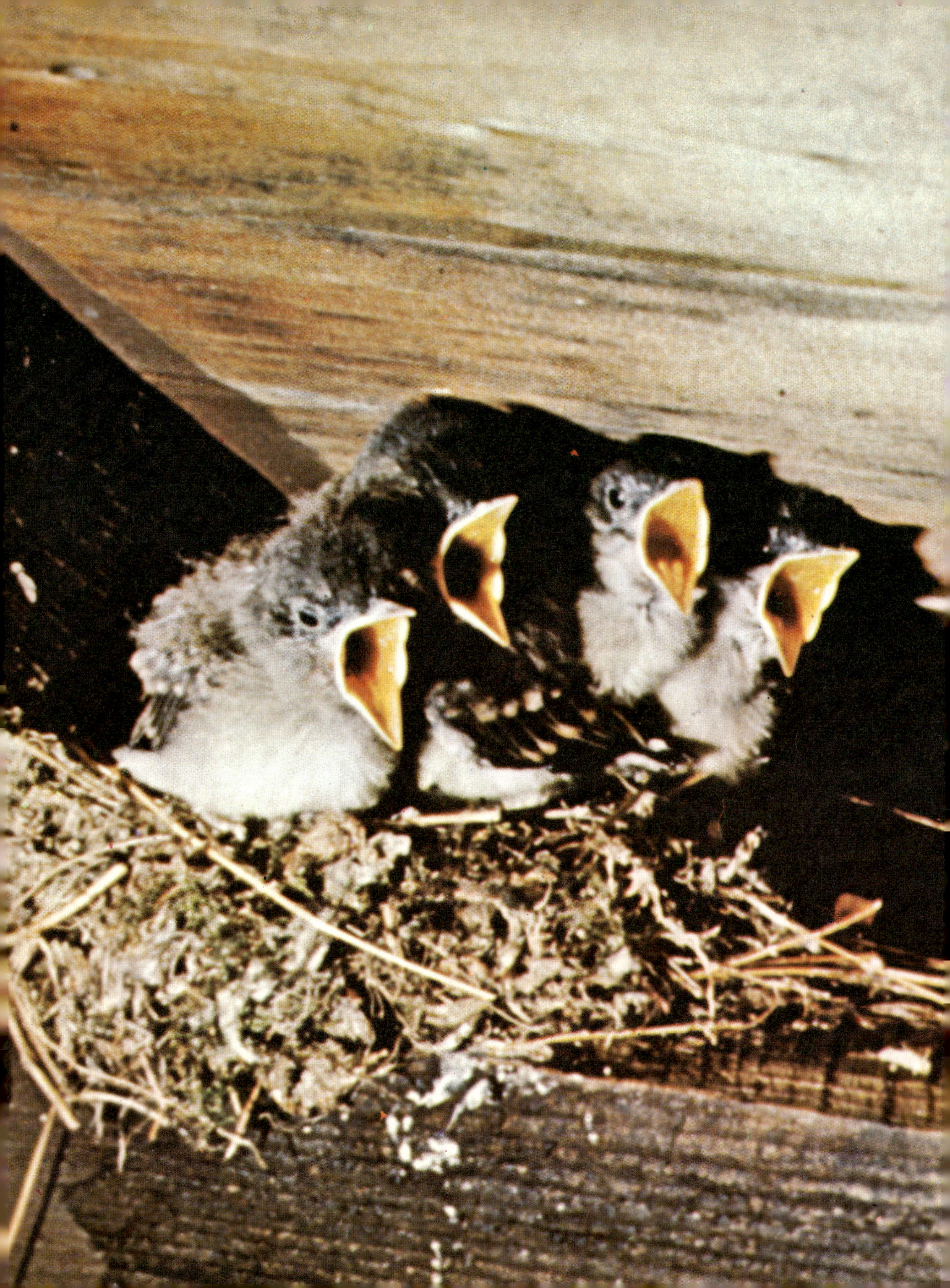

Fledglings trying to fly

European nations had begun to feel a pride in their own countries. This pride made them want to become more powerful and gain control over other areas of the world. By the end of the nineteenth century, most people felt a strong spirit of nationalism (national pride). Smaller countries and areas of the world which were not world powers began to feel national pride too. In Europe and in other parts of the world, smaller countries began to rebel against the big world powers. They were like fledglings in their nest, hungry for freedom. Once they had felt secure in a large empire, now they wanted to try their wings and become nations in their own right.

A nest of hope

When the year 1899 turned into 1900, a new century, the twentieth century had begun. People were very hopeful about peace and progress in the new century. Many wonderful inventions, ideas, and social changes had been hatched throughout the 1800s. The end of the nineteenth century seemed to the peoples in the world to have been the most progressive and exciting yet known. People felt sure that they were handing on a nest of beautiful eggs that would hatch out even better inventions, ideas, and forms of progress.

However, in reality, the nest contained something besides eggs. The threat of war hung over Europe and the world, although people did not realize it at the beginning of the twentieth century. The great powers of Europe were turning into bitter rivals. National spirit in each country made people more ready to fight for their power and pride. The skull of death rested among the eggs lying in the peaceful nest.

Index

A
academies, 81
"accidents", 95
Africa, 152
agrarian (agricultural) revolution, 59
agriculture, 60
Ajaccio, Corsica, 27
Alaska, 105
alliance, 46
aluminium, 93
America, see United States of America
American Revolution, 142
apes, 135
aristocracy, 8, 121
artillery, 30
arts, 81–2
Austria, 28, 46, 95–101

B
Bastille, 17, 19, 21
battles, 30
Belgium, 40
Bismarck, Otto von, 95–101
Black Sea, 93
blockade, 32
bloodshed, 56
bogey-man, 116
Bolivar, Simon, 50
Bonaparte, Louis-Napoleon, 88, 90, 101
Bonaparte, Napoleon, 27–40, 90; defeat of, 36–40; exile of, 39–40
borders, 46
Boston Tea Party, 142
bourgeoisie, 23
brain, 82
Britain, 46, 55
British Empire, 143–9
brotherhood, 19
Budapest, 55

C
cavalry, 30
Charles X, 52
chess, 13, 16

children, 118; living conditions of, 118
citizen, 23, 27, 52
Citizen-King, 52
Civil War, American, 108–9
class, 75
clergy, 8, 13–14
coal, 64; mines, 118
cobwebs, 44–5
codes, 49
collapse of governments, 55
colonies, 142, 150–5
commoners, 52
Congress of Vienna, 46, 49
consent, 45, 49
constitution, French, 14, 19, 45; suspension of, 52
Consul, First, 28
Corsica, 27
cotton, 66, 108
covered wagon, 105
cowboys, 107
craftsmen, 130
crime, 126–7
Crimea, 93
culture, 81
customs, 150

D
Darwin, Charles, 135–6
Declaration of the Rights of Man, 19
Democrats, 107
Denmark, 55
deputies, 52
Descent of Man, The, 136
Directory, the, 27
diseases, 125, 136
divine right to rule, 44, 49
Duke of Orleans, 52, 88

E
economic change, 62
education, 81, 123, 130

Eiffel Tower, 25
Elba, 39
electricity, 133
emblems, 49, 52
Emperor, democratic, 88; of France, 28, 90; of Germany, 101
Empress of India, 147
encephalograph, 82
entertainment, 128–9
Estates, 8–12; 21, 23; General, 13–14
exhibitions, 81, 93
exile of Napoleon, 38–40

F
factories, 64–6
Factory Act, 118
farming, 60
fashion, 8, 93
First Consul, 28
First Estate, 8, 23
fleur-de-lis, 52
freedom, 19, 50, 78; economic, 78
freedom fighters, 50
French Revolution, 17, 19, 21, 25
frontier, American, 105

G
Germany, 49, 95–101
germs, 125, 136
gold, 76
golden laurel, 28
goods, 78, 152
Grand Army, 36–9
Great Britain, 46, 55
guillotine, 25
guns, 152
gymnasiums, 49

H
Hawaii, 105
health, 125, 136
Holland, 38–43
Holstein, 95
Holy Alliance, 46
housing, 71, 123
Hungary, 55

I
idols, 76
immigrants, 112
Indians, American, 105–7
industrial age, 81
Industrial Revolution, 56–88
industrialists, 75, 78
injustice, 17, 107
inventions, 68, 133
Italy, 55, 93
ivy (red), 56

J
Jenner, Edward, 136

L
languages, 150
laurel, golden, 28
laws, 14, 45
learning, 81
leisure time, 128–9
"liberators", 50
liberty, fraternity and equality, 19
Lincoln, Abraham, 109
living conditions, 86, 117–25, 140; of children, 118
Louis XVI, 19
Louis XVIII, 39–40
Louis-Napoleon Bonaparte, see Bonaparte, Louis-Napoleon
Louis-Phillipe, see Duke of Orleans

M
machines, 66
man, 134–6
"man of destiny", 27
manufactured goods, 78
medical aid, 140
Metternich, Prince, 46, 49, 55
Mexico, 93
middle classes, 23, 52, 78–86, 114, 121

monarchy, 16
money, 76
Moscow, 37

N
Napoleon, *see*
   Bonaparte, Napoleon
Napoleonic Empire, 35
National Assembly,
   14–16, 19
nationalism, 88, 155
natural rights, 19, 44–5
navies, 32–3
Nelson, Horatio, 32–3
New York, 112
nobility, French, 8–11,
   13, 14, 23, 121
novel, 85

O
On the Origin of Species,
   135
overcrowding, 71

P
Paris, 17–23, 25
parliament, French, 52
Pasteur, Louis, 136
peace treaties, *see*
   treaties
peasants, 23, 36
Portugal, 50
power, 16, 21, 50
preamble, 19
prisons, 126–7
privileges, 14, 21–3
progress, 114, 117,
   121–3, 138
prosperity, 78, 110
protest, 49
Prussia, 39, 46, 95–101
psychology, 135
Public Health Act, 123
punishment, 126–7

R
railways, 68, 114
reform, 86, 118, 126–7
Reign of Terror, 25
representatives, 52

Republicans, 107
retreat of French Army,
   37–8
Revolution, French,
   17–21, 25, 88
rights, 19, 21, 44–5
riots, 52
Royalty, 13
Russia, 37–9, 46, 55

S
St Helena, 40
salad days, 50
San Martin, José, 50
Schleswig, 95
schools, 81, 130
science, 133–6
sea power, 32–3
Second Empire, 90–3
Second Estate, 8, 21, 23
secret societies, 49
security, 140
self-made man, 75
slavery, 108–9
slums, 71, 123
smallpox, 136
social change, 62, 156
social consciousness,
   114
South America, 50
Spain, 50, 101
specialists, 130
spies, 30, 49
"spinning jenny", 64
Statue of Liberty, 112
steam engine, 62–4, 114
students, 49
subjects, 148
Sultan of Turkey, 93
survival of the fittest,
   136
Sweden, 38–9
symbols, 25, 38–9

T
taxes, 11
telephone, 73
territories, 150–2
terrorism, 25
thinkers, 11, 82

Third Estate, 8, 13–14,
   16, 23
tools, 70
torture, 126–7
Toulon, 27
towns, 66
trade unions, 123
Trafalgar, 32
transport, 68, 114
treaties, 28
tri-colour, 52
Tuileries, 23
Turkey, 93

U
United States of
   America, 103–12, 142
Universal German
   Student Society, 49

V
vaccination, 136
Versailles, 11
Victoria, Queen, 147
Voltaire, 11

W
wars, 46, 152, 156
Washington, D.C., 105
Washington, George,
   142
water power, 62
Waterloo, 40
Watt, James, 64
weaving loom, 64
welfare state, 140
Wellington, Duke of, 40
West, the American,
   105–7
White House, the, 105
wigs, 14
work, 70
working classes, 50, 86,
   117–21
writers, 11, 81